HOW DO YOU
KN●W
IT'S TRUE ?

HOW DO YOU KN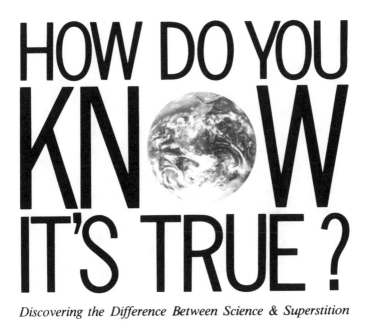OW IT'S TRUE?

Discovering the Difference Between Science & Superstition

HY RUCHLIS

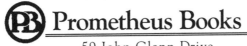 **Prometheus Books**

59 John Glenn Drive
Amherst, New York 14228-2197

Inquiries should be addressed to
Prometheus Books, 59 John Glenn Drive, Amherst, New York 14228–2197.
VOICE: 716–691–0133, ext. 207.
FAX: 716–564–2711.
WWW.PROMETHEUSBOOKS.COM

03 02   6 5 4 3

Library of Congress Cataloging-in-Publication Data

Ruchlis, Hyman.
        How do you know it's true? : discovering the difference between science and superstition / by Hy Ruchlis.
                p.   cm.
        Summary: Discusses the difference between science and superstition, the basic nature of science as a way of thinking, and the ways in which amazing events can be explained rationally.
        ISBN 0–87975–657–8
        1. Science—Methodology—Juvenile literature. 2. Superstitition—Juvenile literature. [1. Science—Methodology. 2. Superstitition.] I. Title.
Q175.2.R83   1991
507.2—dc20   90–28449
                                                                      CIP
                                                                      AC

Printed in the United States of America on acid-free paper

Contents

PART ONE: SUPERSTITION AND
      FAIRY-TALE THINKING

1. Fiction or Fact?   11

2. The Nature of Superstition   15

3. An Experiment with a Superstition   25

4. Astrology: Science or Superstition?   35

PART TWO: SCIENCE AS A WAY OF THINKING

5. How New Facts Are Discovered   47

6. Science and Freedom of Thought   59

7. Developing a Theory: Probability   73

8. Unusual Events: Luck and Chance   83

9. Science Gives Us Real Knowledge   93

10. Science: Past, Present, and Future   101

Acknowledgments

My deepest appreciation goes to my wife, Elsie, who not only undertook many additional family responsibilities that made it possible for me to write this book, but also suggested a number of improvements in the manuscript.

Ruth Handel, who read the manuscript, offered several important ideas that were incorporated into the book.

Last, but not least, granddaughter Kathy Ember, age 13, found a number of explanations in the book that seemed confusing to her and were therefore improved in the final work.

Finally, to my other granddaughters, Julie Ember and Annalisa Ruchlis, and to all other children who were the main motivation for me to write this book—to cope with the confusions of modern life they need to be able to recognize "fairy-tale thinking" and superstition whenever they encounter it.

PART ONE

SUPERSTITION AND FAIRY-TALE THINKING

1

Fiction or Fact?

Do you remember the story of Cinderella? Her fairy godmother waved a magic wand and changed a pumpkin into a coach, some mice into horses, and a rat into a man to drive the coach. Then, with another wave of her wand, she instantly dressed Cinderella in beautiful clothes and glass slippers.

As a child, when this story was read to you, did you wonder how a tiny mouse could be instantly changed into a large horse? Or a small rat changed into a big man?

You knew that this story was a "fairy tale," pure *fiction* that described imaginary people doing *magical* things that could not have happened. What you knew about the real world *contradicted* the events described in the fairy tale.

Children enjoy fairy tales because imagination is stimulated by the game of "Let's Pretend." We encourage the telling and reading of fairy tales because this helps children learn to enjoy books and reading. But as young folk grow older they quickly learn that many of the events said to happen in fairy tales cannot happen in real life.

Not all "fairy tales" are in books. We are all fond of the delightful story of Santa Claus bringing gifts to every child in the world on Christmas eve. Adults know we are playing a game of "Let's Pretend," but many young children think that Santa Claus really exists. They have not yet developed the reasoning power to realize the *contradictions* with reality.

How could just one Santa bring toys for perhaps a billion children everywhere on earth in just one night? How does he get all those toys into one small sleigh? How do those reindeer manage to fly? How does a chubby Santa ever manage to get those bulky toys down the narrow chimneys described in story books, and somehow scramble out again?

As children grow older and gain experience, they begin to understand that events described in the story of Santa Claus contradict what we know about the real world. They come to realize that he is a "symbol" for the joyous season of gift-giving and good will, but does not actually exist.

Any adult who could not tell the difference between fairy-tale fiction and real-world facts would have a very serious problem. If someone insisted he was Napoleon, or that he was made of green cheese, we would immediately send him off to see a psychiatrist. He would need immediate help.

We must be able to know the difference between what is *true*, and what is *false*. But how do we know that what we think is a fact is really so?

FACTS MUST BE BASED ON OBSERVATIONS

Some simple facts are easily *observed* and *checked* by others. For example, if someone tells you that a rubber ball costs one dollar at a local store, it is easy to check that fact by going there and *seeing* it on a price tag, or *hearing* the salesperson say, "It costs a dollar."

Or, if someone tells you that a certain person lives at 65 Cloudburst Street and the phone number is 123-4567, it is not hard to check these facts. You could *look* in the telephone book, or *hear* the person talk on the telephone when you call. You might *check* the address by actually going there to *see* the person.

Anyone can verify such facts by means of observations—by using our senses: sight, hearing, touch, smell, and taste.

Modern business could not exist without such facts as prices, catalog numbers, and descriptions for products; names, addresses, and telephone numbers of customers and suppliers; bills, checks, profits, and money in the bank. There are many billions of such facts, necessary to maintain our modern society.

SOME FACTS ARE HARD TO DISCOVER

However, many kinds of facts, or what we think are facts, are difficult to discover. For example, someone may get a severe pain that he thinks is in his stomach and take some medicine for indigestion. But perhaps what he thinks is a "fact" about the pain "in his stomach" may not be so at all. If the cause of the pain is a heart ailment, or a diseased gall bladder, taking the wrong medicine, or waiting too long to see a doctor, could be fatal.

The pain itself is an observation because it is something that we know exists. We actually *feel* it. But mistakes are easily made when we try to figure out what the observation means. We may reason incorrectly and "jump to a conclusion" that is wrong. For example, someone may feel a pain in the leg and think there is something wrong where the pain is located. The pain may actually be caused by pressure on a nerve in the lower back. In that case, a treatment for the leg is useless, and perhaps harmful.

For such health problems it is best to see doctors who are experts in discovering the causes of illnesses by means of observations. They can then usually prescribe remedies likely to work.

Of course, doctors sometimes make mistakes in judgment. Perhaps the facts are difficult to get or knowledge about some diseases is limited. But what counts is that the facts doctors do know usually enable them to prevent or cure many diseases that once killed many people. As a result, today the average life span is much longer than a century ago.

It has taken centuries for thousands of scientists to find the causes of a great many different diseases. It usually takes many years of research to discover just a single important fact. Then it may take more years of work for others to *verify* it, to be sure it is true and not a mistake in observations or reasoning.

For example, the earliest microscopes in the 1600s revealed the existence of microscopic plants and animals. It took another two centuries before it was proved that many deadly diseases are caused by different kinds of these microorganisms. Doctors did not even know that they had to wash their hands before treating different patients in hospitals, just to remove deadly germs. They actually caused many deaths just by transmitting germs when touching people with infected hands.

Discovery of new facts in science is not simple or easy. It takes careful observation and lots of hard work.

Wrong ideas tend to continue for many years, often for centuries. But gradually, over the years, we have learned how to tell the difference between fact and fiction. We have been steadily improving the way we uncover new facts, not known before.

We call that method of discovery "science." Science is much more than the *facts* that make up today's knowledge about the nature of the world in which we live. It is really a new and different *way of thinking,*—a way of knowing how to find new facts and prove them true. This scientific way of thinking has transformed our world and made it very different from what it was just a few centuries ago.

This book is about the methods of science, the way it differs from superstitious "fairy-tale" ways of thinking, how it has changed our world, and how we might use it to solve many of the difficult problems of the world we live in today.

But first, let's go back three centuries, to the year 1692, to see how the wrong, superstitious way of thinking of olden times was misused to execute innocent people in our country, wrongly accused of what was considered to be the "crime" of "witchcraft."

2

The Nature of Superstition

In 1692 a mysterious sickness began to spread in the town of Salem, Massachusetts. Eight girls had frequent "convulsive fits" in which they thrashed about wildly while moaning, crying, and babbling. During those fits they had hallucinations in which they imagined strange things happening.

People in the community were frightened. If eight girls could get such a scary disease, then anyone else might get it, too. Parents began to worry about the safety of their own children.

Physicians were called in, but in those days they knew very little about illnesses. They found this one especially mystifying. However, one physician wondered if the convulsive fits might have been caused by "witchcraft."

WITCHCRAFT! This superstitious idea struck terror into the hearts of people. Word spread rapidly that there was a witch among them. Perhaps a gang of witches, possessed by the devil, were casting evil spells on the girls. Driven by ignorant fear, the townspeople started a "witchhunt" to find the witches in their midst.

During their babbling the girls would sometimes utter the names of people they knew. The townspeople grasped these flimsy bits of "evidence" as clues to who might be witches. They put anyone named by the girls into jail. Soon there were 150 innocent people awaiting trial for the imagined crime of witchcraft, punishable by death!

They were neighbors of the girls, farmers, storekeepers, housewives, servants, a former minister, and even parents of friends. The people of Salem had been driven wild with fear by a *superstition* about witchcraft that was totally false.

The Governor of Massachusetts appointed some judges to decide which of the people in jail were the witches, and which were not.

How did the judges decide? They used a "test of touch." The accused person had to touch one of the girls while she was having a fit. If the fit stopped immediately this was "proof" that the accused person controlled it, was therefore a witch, and had to be sentenced to death. However, if the fit did not stop then the accused person was considered innocent. (Fig. 2.1)

Figure 2.1. In 1692, during the Salem witch trials, accused people were judged guilty of being witches and executed if a girl's convulsive fit stopped when touched by the person on trial. (Drawing by Albert Sarney)

The judges tried to be merciful. They spared the lives of convicted "witches" if they confessed to the crime of witchcraft. As you might expect, many of the innocent people who were convicted, "confessed" to save their lives. Nineteen of them, however, refused to lie and paid for their honesty and bravery with death by hanging.

This terrible tragedy occurred only because people believed in the false superstition of witchcraft. Witches were imagined to be making people sick by using magical ceremonies, perhaps by uttering special words to cast evil spells on people.

Today, physicians know far more about the causes of disease than in 1692. Several possible explanations have been proposed for the strange illness that afflicted the eight girls.

They might have had a disease known today as "convulsive ergotism." It is caused by a poisonous substance in a microscopic plant, a "fungus" known as "ergot." This fungus grows on crops such as rye, used for making bread. Eating bread containing ergot might have caused the girls to have those fits and hallucinations.

Another possible explanation is that the events in Salem were caused by "mass hysteria." There are examples today of large groups of children, and sometimes adults, who become so anxious and fearful about some reported illness that they imagine they have it, too. The eight girls might have seen or heard about others having fits and their vivid imaginations might have caused them to behave the same way.

It is possible that some, or all the girls, were playing a monstrous trick on grownups by pretending to have fits and hallucinations. Perhaps they enjoyed having the power of life and death over all those innocent grownups.

SUPERSTITIONS TODAY

A superstition is a belief that is held despite evidence that it is not true.

Superstitions are based on the belief that some people, plants, animals, planets, stars, words, numbers, or special things have *magical* powers. They are supposed to be able to do astonishing things that no one truly *observes* happening anywhere, although many people *imagine* they are happening. These superstitions *contradict* what we know about the real world.

Superstitions are examples of *fairy-tale thinking*. But, unlike fairy tales, which people know are imaginative fiction, superstitions are wrongly believed to be true.

Scientific thinking is very different. We seek facts and explanations of events based on careful *observations* and logical *reasoning* that must be *checked* by repeated trials to try to eliminate the errors that often occur. Then the facts have to be *verified* by other careful observers before being accepted as true.

This is not an easy or quick process and mistakes are often

made. Very often it takes years of work by many people to reach the point where facts and conclusions are considered to be true. Because mistakes or exaggerations are easy to make we must be ready to correct, or even change our ideas about facts as new information becomes available.

In sharp contrast, superstitious belief reflects a lazy way of thinking. Superstitious people just *assume* the "facts" and often believe whatever they *imagine* to be true. The way this happens will be described in chapter 4 when the superstition of astrology is analyzed in detail.

Today, polls show that, despite all our scientific knowledge, one person in seven in the United States believes in superstitions like the one about witchcraft. One in four people believe in the superstition of astrology and more than 1,000 newspapers encourage this superstition by publishing "horoscopes" which supposedly predict for people of different birth dates what they should or should not expect to happen to them.

Some people have formed groups that perform special witchcraft ceremonies. There have been reports of animals sacrificed during such events to ward off bad luck, or to try to accomplish some other desired goal.

In one tragic case a woman whose child was ill was told by a person, who claimed to be able to heal sickness by superstition, that a demon had possessed the child, causing the disease. The remedy proposed was to starve the demon by depriving the child of food. The mother actually did so, and the child starved to death!

This poor woman was punished with a jail sentence of four years. The real cause of her child's death was ignorance, which led her to believe in an ancient superstition about demons causing illness.

Superstitious belief in witchcraft is more widespread in countries with many uneducated people and few modern physicians. People then rely on traditional "witch doctors" or "medicine men" who try to cure diseases with ceremonies and magic that are supposed to drive out imaginary demons thought to cause disease.

Witch doctors collect things like skins of snakes and frogs, skulls or bones of animals, unusual rocks, carvings of animals, and other objects, all supposed to have magical powers to cure people. They may use such materials as magical objects in their ceremonies, waving them around the sick person as they utter magic words and perhaps dance or make special motions. (Fig 2.2)

Figure 2.2. This witch doctor performs a ceremony to drive out the demon, imagined to be causing an illness. Since most sick people get better, ceremony or not, the witch doctor takes credit for his "successes," even though undeserved. (American Museum of Natural History)

Scientists are careful not to reject everything witch doctors do as worthless in treating illness and disease. Witch doctors often make medicines from parts of different plants or animals. Some of these medicines have been found to be useful in curing diseases.

For example, quinine, the main medicine used by modern

physicians for treating malaria, was originally discovered by Indian medicine men in South America. They made it from the bark of cinchona trees. Also, an important tranquilizer to make people calmer was originally used by witch doctors in Asia. Other medicines used today were discovered in a similar way.

Of course, performing magical ceremonies and uttering special words do not stop germs from invading the body, nor do they cure vitamin deficiencies. However, ceremonies are often better than doing nothing because they give sick people the feeling that something is being done to help them. They feel more optimistic, and this mental attitude has been found to be helpful to the body in fighting off some diseases.

Since people recover from most diseases by themselves, imagined "cures" by ceremonies and magic words seem to "prove" that the superstitions are effective. This is also true for some medicines sold today in pharmacies. When people get better, with or without the medicine, they may mistakenly think that the medicine did it.

The best way to find out if a medicine really works is to test it with a *controlled* experiment. A number of sick people are given the medicine being tested, while others are given false medicines called *placebos* (pronounced pla-SEE-bose), which are harmless substitutes. Careful records of medical examinations are kept to see how these people recover from the illness. The medicine is considered to work if many more patients getting the medicine recover, or do so faster.

In such experiments it is best if the doctors or nurses actually giving the medical examinations do not know which patients are getting the real medicines and which are getting the placebos. People doing experiments often want the experiment to "succeed." If they know which patients are getting the real medicine, they may be *biased* and slant their observations to favor the outcome they want.

The people getting the placebos serve as the *control* group that gives us a way to compare what happens with and without the medicine.

Such experiments are very expensive because many people are involved, they often take a long time, and costly measuring instruments may have to be used. But it is the best way to be sure that any medicine or other treatment actually works.

The lesson we have learned from witch doctors is that every belief we think is a superstition should not be automatically rejected. We should examine each superstition carefully to see if there is some truth to it. The *evidence* for or against it should determine whether we consider it true or false.

OTHER SUPERSTITIONS

People today sometimes do or say things because of customs based on ancient superstitions. For example, a friend may say something like, "I hope it doesn't rain Saturday and spoil our picnic." Then she interrupts the conversation, raps the wooden table with her knuckles, and says, "Knock on wood." Why did she do that?

Your friend does not realize it, but she is knocking on wood because people in olden times believed there were elves with magical powers trapped in wooden objects in our homes. They were imagined to have originally lived in trees in the woods. But when trees were chopped down and made into furniture, the elves were supposed to still be in the wood, right in our homes. Ancient people were afraid that the elves were angry for being deprived of their beautiful homes in the woods, and were just waiting for a chance to get even.

Today no one ever thinks about the elves, or explains how they manage to understand English, or why we never see them. But when your friend knocks on wood, it is as if she is really assuming, like people long ago, that some invisible elf trapped in the furniture has heard her remark about rain spoiling her picnic.

"Aha," he is imagined to think. "Now I have a way to punish those mean people. I'll use my magical powers to make it rain on Saturday and spoil their picnic."

The procedure of saying, "Knock on wood," and then actually knocking on something made of wood is supposed to be a magical way of telling the elf, "Don't spoil our picnic or we'll punish you. Remember, we could make things difficult for you by chopping up this table and burning it in the fireplace."

This superstitious custom makes as much sense as expecting a fairy godmother to wave a wand and instantly create a limousine and chauffeur to drive us to a big party.

Today we know that saying words cannot stop any illness from developing. But in olden times people believed in the superstition that saying the right words had the magical ability to make things happen. A witch was supposed to be able to cast an evil spell by uttering special curses. Special words, like "abracadabra," were imagined to have magical effects such as opening locked doors without keys or releasing genies from bottles.

BLACK CATS AND OTHER SUPERSTITIONS

Some people still believe that a black cat crossing one's path brings "bad luck." To avoid this "bad luck" a superstitious person might turn around and go back, or go another way.

Superstitious people may do strange things to cancel "bad luck." An old-time remedy for a black cat's "bad luck" was to rotate one's hat around on the head, take nine steps and then rotate the hat back to where it was before. No one ever explains how they know the superstition is true, or how the black color of a cat's fur could magically cause someone to perhaps fall and break a leg, or why the rotated hat remedy is supposed to work.

In fact, people think they "know" that the superstition is true because they were told about it by others. When we try to track down who started this superstition we find that it goes all the way back into ancient times, without a shred of reliable evidence that it is true.

In England the superstition is just the opposite, with black cats imagined to produce "good luck," not bad! Some theaters actually keep black cats to bring them "good luck" in performances and newspaper reviews. How could a black cat be "bad luck" in the United States and bring "good luck" when sent across the ocean?

The superstition may have arisen from the fact that in our society the color black is associated with funerals and death. Halloween drawings of witches usually show them with black hats, and often black cats are nearby. Perhaps the black cat is supposed to be a witch in disguise, or some kind of spy or helper for the witch. It may therefore have been imagined to possess the same magical ability to cause harm.

A similar superstition is that breaking a mirror brings "bad luck." This belief is based on the mysterious way people see their images in a mirror. In olden times people did not know about the way light is reflected by a mirror to produce an image. The mirror image seemed to appear as if by magic. When we

Figure 2.3. The superstition about a broken mirror causing "bad luck" probably arose because of the mysterious way an image appears behind a mirror, even though nothing is actually observed to be there. Perhaps people thought a person's spirit could not return once the mirror was broken. (Drawing by Albert Sarney)

look for it behind the mirror nothing is there. (Fig. 2.3)

Perhaps the mirror was imagined to mysteriously capture a person's "spirit," which could then not return to the owner of the image when the mirror was broken. The grumpy spirit would thereafter try to get even by magically causing misfortunes to happen to the person who broke it.

There is a superstition that stepping on an ant brings rain. Considering how many people everywhere on earth step on ants all day long, it ought to be raining all the time. This conclusion clearly contradicts our experience.

"Voodoo," a superstitious form of magic, is practiced in some countries today, even in the United States. One of its beliefs is that a person can be harmed at a distance by using magical procedures. One method is to stick pins into a doll representing the person to be harmed. This is supposed to cause that person to get sick or die.

Unfortunately, this can really harm intended victims who believe in the superstition and are told that evil spells have been put on them. Just worrying about an evil spell could make an intended victim sick, and perhaps even die.

Belief in superstitions is widespread in countries where people are poorly educated and is greatly weakened when people become educated. But even in nations where everybody goes to school some people are still superstitious. Superstitions take a very long time to die out.

Scientific thinking has gradually developed mainly during the past five centuries. It has transformed the world by sweeping away most of the superstitions that prevented people from learning about the world in which we live.

Could we use scientific thinking to test a superstition to find out if there is any truth to it? The next chapter describes how that could be done.

3

An Experiment with a Superstition

You step into the elevator of a tall building. The door closes and up you go. You watch the lights that show the number of each floor that is passed: 1, 2, 3, 4, 5, 6, 7, 8, 9, 10, 11, 12 . . . and what's this? There's 12, then 14, but no 13!

Did somebody make a mistake in counting? No. The thirteenth floor is really there, right above the twelfth floor. It's just that the real thirteenth floor of about half the tall buildings in our country have been deliberately marked 14 instead of 13.

Why has that been done?

There is an ancient superstition that the number 13 brings "bad luck." Some people actually believe in that superstition today and therefore do not rent, buy, or visit apartments or offices on floors marked 13. (Figure 3.1)

Some people who are not superstitious may also not rent or buy on the thirteenth floor because they know that superstitious people would not work or visit there.

A strange thing about this superstition is that every building with more than twelve floors has a thirteenth floor. Painting the number 14 on floor 13 doesn't change it from being the thirteenth floor. So why should just a wrong number 14 on a wall make any difference? This logic is somehow lost on superstitious people. Someone told them that the *number* 13 brings "bad luck" so they simply believe it without question.

Figure 3.1. Some superstitious people will not live, work, or visit a floor marked 13 because they believe it would cause them "bad luck." Builders sometimes mark the real 13th floor with a false 14 so that superstitious people will not have to worry that the number 13 will haunt them. (Drawing by Albert Sarney)

"CARDSTACKING" THE EVIDENCE FOR A SUPERSTITION

Superstitious people say they "know" that the number 13 is unlucky because they claim to have observed examples when it seems to have been true. "Last month Sam Bungling, who lives in apartment 1303, fell off a bicycle and broke his arm. Then last week Mary Contrary, from 1307, had her car stolen. And don't forget, Bill Barker, in apartment 1310, was bitten by a dog yesterday. I told him not to rent that apartment on the thirteenth floor."

Believers in the superstition claim that such "anecdotal evidence" (based on "anecdotes": stories about events) is based on observations. But the mere listing of misfortunes for people living or working on a thirteenth floor does not *prove* that they are the result of special "bad luck," because *everyone* has some misfortunes, including those living on any other floors. We could give as many examples of misfortunes on those floors as on floor 13.

We can't tell whether the people living or working on a floor marked 13 are more "unlucky" than people living on other floors unless we can show this by careful observations. An experiment, based on a detailed investigation, would have to be performed.

When people try to "prove" superstitions, or even opinions, with anecdotal evidence they often make a common error in reasoning called *cardstacking*. This word comes from the way some gamblers prepare ("stack") cards in advance of a game in special ways that give them better chances to win.

People cardstack the evidence when they look for, or show, only those examples that are in favor of whatever they want to "prove," while hiding or ignoring all the examples that show it to be untrue. (Figure 3.2)

Some people deliberately cardstack evidence to mislead others. But more often, people are so eager to "prove" them-

Figure 3.2. Evidence is often "cardstacked" by presenting only the facts FOR while hiding or suppressing the facts AGAINST. People often fool themselves by ignoring or rejecting facts that may show their opinions to be wrong. (Drawing by Albert Sarney)

selves right in their opinions that they ignore the evidence showing them to be wrong.

AN EXPERIMENT TO FIND THE TRUTH ABOUT 13

Could we do a scientific experiment to see if there is any truth to the superstition that living on a floor marked thirteen brings "bad luck?" What would we have to do?

Suppose a student named Eddie does such an experiment for his science project. He selects a tall building with a thirteenth floor and decides to interview people living on that floor. He also needs a "control" for purposes of comparison, perhaps the twelfth flooor, to see which one has people with more "bad luck." He plans to find out about the amount of "bad luck" by interviewing everyone on both floors.

Eddie starts by ringing the bell for apartment 1301. A middle-aged man appears. "Yeah. Whaddaya want?"

Eddie explains his science project and asks the man if he will cooperate by listing the misfortunes he has had recently. The man glares at Eddie.

"I ain't got no time for such nonsense. I'm watching a football game." SLAM goes the door. Now Eddie can't go there any more. He crosses 1301 off the list.

This is serious. Missing one, or several apartments, distorts the comparison. Gruff people like the man in 1301 may be angry at the world because they have had a lot of misfortunes and don't want to talk about them. In that case Eddie would be missing many examples of "bad luck" and his records would be incomplete.

In apartment 1302 he finds a nice lady who says, "That's a great idea. Sure, I'll be glad to help you with your project. Come in and have some cookies and soda."

She begins a long account of lots of little misfortunes. "Let's see. On Monday I scraped my arm and it bled, so I washed it with peroxide, then put on a Band-Aid. And last Wednesday my uncle Pete had a pain in his stomach. Would you believe that the doctor sent him to the hospital right away? Thought he might be having a heart attack. So they took a cardiogram, but found nothing wrong. But they are keeping him for observation for a few days. . . ." And so on for half an hour.

CAN WE MEASURE "BAD LUCK?"

That night Eddie tries to figure out what to do with his scribbled notes about a number of interviews. He enounters a serious problem. Which is a worse misfortune, a broken leg or pneumonia? How should he compare one person's loss of a job with getting a divorce? Or losing $1,000 in a bad investment? Or learning that a very good friend died?

Researchers doing interviews of events involving what people say or do often set up a rating system from one to ten, which helps them compare answers or results. Eddie does the same by rating the smallest misfortune as one and the worst a ten.

What rating does he assign to the misfortune of a broken leg? Five? Seven? Nine? How does he take into account the severity of the break, when some legs are as good as new in a few months, while others cause permanent crippling?

What rating is assigned to losing a wallet with $100? This is a big misfortune to someone with a large family who barely earns enough money to get by. But it's practically no misfortune to a millionaire. How does Eddie find out how rich or poor the loser may be?

Different people are also likely to rate misfortunes differently. Someone who has never known poverty may not give a high rating for the loss of $100, easily replaced (for him) by going to the bank. A poor person doing the rating is likely to be more sympathetic and rate the loss higher on the scale.

Here's another problem: Eddie found ten people reporting minor cuts, easily fixed with Band-Aids. He gives each of these a rating of one, for a total of ten. But then he also rated a death in the family, reported by one person, with the highest value of ten. Yet that death is clearly a lot worse than ten separate Band-Aid cuts, also worth a total of ten.

For these reasons the rating system for misfortunes is said to be "subjective," and not "objective."

SUBJECTIVE OR OBJECTIVE?

Judgments are *subjective* when they depend on differing opinions, beliefs, and personal experiences. Eddie's rating system is clearly very subjective. If Elsie, Bobby, or Sally were rating the same misfortunes, each one would probably assign very different ratings. Ratings of "bad luck," based on what people tell us about their misfortunes, are certainly very subjective.

On the other hand, ratings are said to be *objective* if they are not based on personal feelings or prejudice, but on some kind of easily repeated measurement that enables everyone to assign practically the same rating.

For example, ten people trying to judge the length of a room just by sight would give many different estimates. But a measuring tape would enable all to agree on the length within a fraction of an inch.

On the other hand, no instrument can measure the amount of "bad luck" because it is too vague and *abstract*. It has no length, width, height, volume, weight, or color that can be *measured*. We can't see it, hear it, touch it, smell it, or taste it. It is not a *thing* but an abstract *idea*.

Many important, hard-to-measure ideas about the world are very abstract: good, bad, better, worse, luck, democracy, freedom, love, hate, jealousy, and lots more. To get some kind of measurement to compare good and bad luck we have to invent a tricky, subjective rating system that depends on the ideas people have.

The numbers people assign to ratings are deeply affected by their *prejudices* (pre-judgments.) Their ratings would be *biased* (slanted) in favor of what they think is better or worse. In such cases people tend to "cardstack" their records by not noting misfortunes they think are unimportant.

Cardstacking also occurs if people have strong opinions about the outcome of an experiment. For example, if Eddie believes that 13 is an unlucky number, he may give higher ratings to similar misfortunes on floor 13 than to those on other floors.

People are usually not aware of bias in their strongly held opinions. It is *subconscious* (below the level of consciousness, or awareness). They feel better if their opinions are shown to be right, and feel badly if shown to be wrong. So they often "see what they want to see." In such cases a subjective experiment to see if the superstition about "bad luck" on the thirteenth floor is true, or not, is likely to end up "proving" whatever the person wants to prove.

One way for Eddie to reduce the effect of his bias would be to have several other people rate the misfortunes on the two floors, without knowing whether they occurred on floor 12 or 13. But this greatly complicates his experiment.

WHAT DO THE RATINGS MEAN?

There are still more problems after the ratings of "bad luck" are assigned. Suppose Eddie adds up the ratings of all misfortunes for each floor and finds the total for floor 12 to be 217, while that for floor 13 is 249.

To see how much greater 249 is than 217, he divides 249 by 217 and gets 1.15. This is the same as saying 249 is 15% greater than 217. Does this "prove" that people living on floor 13 had 15% more misfortunes than for floor 12, and therefore had more "bad luck?"

No. There is too much *variation* with only ten families on each floor, and only for one month. If Eddie were to conduct interviews for another month or in another building, the misfortunes would certainly be different and the totals might go the other way, with floor 12 getting the higher total.

There is some safety in having a greater number of interviews, in more buildings, in different places, and for a longer period of time.

How many interviews are enough? Scientists use a kind of mathematics called *statistics* to guide them in judging how often they should repeat a measurement or rating to get enough observations to make a proper judgment.

You can see that it would require a lot of time and money to do an experiment properly to find out if people on floor 13 really have more "bad luck."

No one has ever done this properly for the superstition about "bad luck" on floors marked 13, partly because of the time, effort, and cost. But suppose someone actually did this. Those who disagree with the conclusions could find plenty of reasons for saying that the experiment is unscientific because the ratings are so subjective, and therefore it doesn't prove anything.

HOW TO SHOW THAT A SUPERSTITION IS NOT TRUE

Although probably no one has done an experiment to find out if there is more "bad luck" on the thirteenth floor, there is good evidence to show that the general superstition about number 13 is not true.

Records are kept by hospitals, police, fire and health departments, and insurance companies, for many kinds of misfortunes: fires, crimes, diseases, deaths, accidents in homes, car and airplane crashes. This information is quite reliable because it is based on objective *observations* by physicians, firemen, policemen, and other officials. These people have no reason to be biased about noting that somebody died, or that people were injured in auto accidents, and on what dates they happened.

As a result, we can easily test the truth of a common superstition about 13, that Friday the 13th (or any other thirteenth day of the month) is unlucky. We can simply total all the deaths, or accidents, or fires, or illnesses, or crimes on different days of each month and compare these completely objective numbers.

These official records show that no more misfortunes occur on Friday the 13th, or on any other thirteenth day of the month, than on other days. This is strong evidence that the superstition about the number 13 being "unlucky" is not true.

USING OUR REASONING POWER

We can also use *logical reasoning* to show that the superstition about 13 is very unlikely to be true. Let's ask an important scientific question that superstitious people ignore: *How is the number 13 supposed to cause misfortunes for people living on a thirteenth floor?*

Suppose someone who is superstitious gets off the elevator on a thirteenth floor and sees a big 13 on the wall. Does that number 13 somehow have invisible eyes that see and recognize a victim? Does the invisible spirit of that ghostly 13 then follow the victim around for the next few months? Does it arrange to have a banana peel on some steps to make the victim fall and break a leg to give him some "bad luck"? (Figure 3.3)

Just asking these questions tells us how silly the superstition is. There is nothing we have ever seen, heard, felt, smelled, or tasted, nothing we can observe, that could explain how a mere number 13 on the wall could do all those magical things.

Such superstitions contradict what we know about the way the real world works. It is an example of fairy-tale thinking.

For that reason we are quite sure that the superstition about 13 and "bad luck" is very unlikely to be true, as much as we can know anything else in this complicated world.

Other superstitions about "bad luck" or "good luck" can

Figure 3.3. Belief in the superstition that the number 13 causes "bad luck" implies that some kind of ghostly "spirit" of 13 follows people around and arranges some kind of misfortune to occur. There is no observable evidence that this is so. (Drawing by Albert Sarney)

be analyzed in much the same way, by means of reasoning, as we have done for the superstition about 13.

HOW SUPERSTITIONS CAN HARM US

There is a way for the number 13 to harm a person. Suppose someone who strongly believes in the superstition about 13 causing "bad luck" happens to visit a floor marked 13. The fear that the evil spirit of 13 would pursue its victim, and inevitably cause harm, could make a believer nervous and accident-prone (likely to have accidents). Little misfortunes are then likely to be exaggerated and imagined to be big ones. Some people can worry themselves into illness, even death, by imagining the worst.

In one recent trial for murder, a son was accused of killing his father who had tyrannized the family and friends with the superstitious belief that he had an evil spirit in an urn. The reason the son gave for the murder is that he had to free the family from the terrible power of the evil spirit that they were convinced was in the urn.

Even with the tyrannical father gone the family did not dare to throw it into a garbage dump because they believed the magical powers of the evil spirit would somehow find a way to harm them.

The family solved their problem with the evil spirit by calling in an "exorcist" to get rid of the spirit by saying the right magic words and declaring it dead. Only then did they feel safe. Meanwhile, of course, the father was dead and the son was in jail awaiting his trial for murder.

The best remedy for such fearful thinking is the knowledge that superstitions about "bad luck" or "good luck" are not true. There is no reliable evidence that there are invisible, supernatural spirits that can do magical things that contradict what we know about the real world.

Of course, most people do not think that they could ever be taken in by such superstitious beliefs. But just a minute! Polls show that one out of four people in the United States believes in another superstition called astrology. Widespread belief in this superstition is also shown by the fact that over 1,000 newspapers in our country publish columns giving daily "horoscopes" that claim to tell people what kinds of events are likely to happen to them in the future, according to their dates of birth.

How do we know that astrology is a superstition? The next chapter explains how we can analyze what astrologers say to show that their beliefs are based on superstition.

4

Astrology: Science or Superstition?

Polls have shown that about one person in four in the United States believes in astrology. Many of them read the daily horoscopes in newspapers and try to follow the advice in those columns. In addition, many books on the subject are published and sold, and some people even pay astrologers a good deal of money to prepare personal horoscopes to help them make important decisions.

Astrologers who prepare these horoscopes say that what they do is good "science," based on "facts." They claim to be able to tell from any person's time and date of birth what kind of character he or she has as an adult. They also declare that they can predict for anybody on earth whether a particular time is "favorable" or "unfavorable" for different kinds of activities people want to undertake. For example, they advise people if any chosen day or time of day is good for a marriage ceremony, starting a business, going on a trip, or for anything else.

Astrologers claim they can do all this by making a "horoscope" for each time and place. They use astronomical tables to figure out exactly where the sun, moon, planets, and constellations were, or will be, in the sky for the particular moment and place. Then they apply very complicated rules of astrology to predict if the luck for the activity in question would be good or bad. If they decide that the moment is not a good one, they claim to be able to tell what time of day, or other days, would be better.

This would be a marvelous service if true. So it is important to answer the question, "Is astrology really science, and can it predict good or back luck for any activity anyone is planning to undertake?"

IS ASTROLOGY TRUE?

A good way to answer such a question is to analyze what astrologers say and do. Let's do this for a famous astrologer, Joan Quigley, who for many years prepared horoscopes for well-known actors and actresses. For six years she was paid a large fee by Nancy Reagan, wife of President Reagan, to prepare horoscopes for many of the president's important appointments.

We know this happened because Nancy Reagan says so in her book *My Turn.* Joan Quigley confirms this in her own book *What Does Joan Say?*

Consider just one of many examples Quigley describes of the kinds of changes she says she made in the president's schedule of important appointments.

In 1987 President Reagan arranged to go to Bitberg, Germany, for a wreath-laying ceremony to honor the memory of Germans who died in World War II. This visit became controversial and Mrs. Reagan was worried, not only about the president's safety, but also about bad publicity. She asked Quigley to check the president's planned schedule and tell her if any changes should be made to avoid "bad luck."

The ceremony had been scheduled for early in the morning. Quigley explains in her book how she prepared a horoscope for the scheduled time and decided that it was not a good-luck moment for the ceremony. She says that at 11:45 A.M. the planets and stars were in a much more "favorable" position for the ceremony. So, she says she insisted that the president's assistant change the time, even though that was difficult to do.

In her book she explains why she made that change:

At the time I chose, the Sun, which ruled the event itself, was in a very elevated position in the 10th house of great prominence and prestige. The sun and the proud, honorable and dignified Leo Ascendant described the nature of the event. Jupiter, the planet of benevolence and good will, represented the public. Two planets in the 9th house indicated global attention. And Mars in the 10th showed a kind of victory.

This way of deciding on a "best" time for the president's ceremony raises many questions:

Why should the sun high in the sky ("in a very elevated position"), and in a certain part of the sky ("10th house"), give the president's ceremony "great prominence and prestige"?

Does the sun have a brain that can understand what is happening on earth at a ceremony in a certain place called Bitberg? Does the sun do the same for all the billions of other human events taking place everywhere on earth at the same time?

Why should a chance collection of separate stars in a constellation called Leo, thousands of billions of miles away, be "proud, honorable and dignified." How could these enormously distant stars "describe the nature" of our president's ceremony in Germany?

How does the planet Jupiter bestow "benevolence and good will," or "represent the public" for a ceremony in Bitberg, Germany, hundreds of millions of miles away? Where did Jupiter get that power? How does it transmit this "benevolence and good will" to earth?

The president's ceremony was already getting top billing on TV and radio programs throughout the world. So, why should "two planets in the 9th house" give it any more "global attention" than it had? And how does Mars give the president's ceremony "victory," whatever that means?

Astrologers do not ask or answer such difficult "why" questions because they are just blindly following the rules of a kind of very complicated game called "astrology"—somewhat like Monopoly. They learned the rules of this game by reading books or going to special schools. Nobody writing these astrology books, or teaching astrology courses, bothers to ask such questions or tries to answer them the way scientists do: by means of careful investigations, usually with experiments.

Most of the rules were invented by astrologers who lived more than 2,000 years ago. Ever since, other astrologers have been blindly following those rules without bothering to prove that what they are doing is true or false! Some of the more creative ones invent their own rules, put them into books, and then teach them to others.

ASTROLOGERS DO NOT UNDERSTAND
WHAT A FACT IS

Consider Quigley's statement that "the Sun . . . was . . . in the 10th house of great prominence and prestige." And then she writes, "Two planets in the 9th house indicated global attention. And Mars in the 10th showed a kind of victory."

What are these "houses" in the sky that Quigley thinks are so important? They are just one of the many kinds of invented rules of the game, imaginary sections of the entire sky from north to south. Most astrologers divide the sky into 12 such "houses," but some have imagined there to be 8, 20, 24, or other numbers of sections.

Using fairy-tale thinking, with no evidence at all, they have imagined each house to have some control over an aspect of human life. Astrologers differ in what they imagine belongs in each house. In the 12-house system that Quigley follows, the First House is imagined to influence human personality and temperament. The Second House takes care of possessions and feelings. Other houses deal with travel, or family, or public affairs, etc.

As the earth rotates on its axis the sky appears to revolve around us once every day, wherever we happen to be. Astrologers imagine that the sun, moon, planets, and constellations each steadily move from one house into the next. When the sun or moon, or a planet or constellation, crosses the fence (boundary) between one house and the next it leaves behind the qualities of the house it was in and picks up those of the new house.

There have been as many as 50 different systems of houses in the sky. Any astrologer can imagine his or her own number of houses and what each should mean. But no one does any controlled experiments to find out if their imaginary houses in the sky really do affect people as they claim. With this fairy-tale thinking, whatever any astrologer imagines to be true is assumed to be true.

Figure 4.1 illustrates how silly this fairy-tale kind of thinking really is. Should anyone delay a trip until the sun appears to move into an imaginary "house" in the sky that is supposed to control everybody's luck while traveling? Since there is no evidence whatsoever that any such "house" exists, why should anyone believe it?

Figure 4.1.
Millie: "Why don't we start on our vacation trip."
Billie: "My astrologer told me to wait until the sun gets into the House of Travel, or we'll run into bad luck."
Millie: "Why didn't we leave an hour ago when it was in the house of wealth?"

ANIMALS IN THE CONSTELLATIONS?

Let's analyze why Quigley thinks that "the proud, honorable and dignified Leo Ascendant described the nature of the event."

Leo is the name of a constellation. The word "Leo" comes from the word "lion" in Latin, an ancient language of the Romans. They had borrowed the idea of a lion in the sky from a Greek myth. It seems that Orion, a mythical hunter, performed the difficult feat of slaying a dangerous lion in the ancient forest of Nimea. Jupiter, the chief Roman god at that time, was so impressed that he honored Orion by permanently fastening the dead lion to the sky as stars in the constellation called Leo.

The arrangement of stars in most constellations does not have the slightest resemblance to the people, animals, or objects that ancient astrologers imagined them to be. For example, in Figure 4.2, which shows how the stars in Leo appear to us, do you see anything that looks like a lion, or anything else?

After ancient astrologers had invented the name Leo (the lion) for this constellation, their vivid imaginations were put

Figure 4.2. This diagram shows the arrangement of bright stars in the constellation called Leo (meaning lion in Latin.) Do you see any lion in the accidental arrangement of stars, as ancient astrologers imagined they saw? When today's astrologers make horoscopes they assume that this ancient superstition is true, although they deny being superstitious. (Drawing by Albert Sarney)

to work dreaming up what kind of influences on luck this lion would have on the lives of *all* people on our distant earth.

They used their favorite method of reasoning by *analogy.* If two different things are alike in some way, then they *might* be alike in other ways. However, astrologers forget the "might be" and take it to mean "must be." They abuse this method of reasoning by analogy so badly, by changing "might" into "must," that we may describe it as *stretched analogy.*

In olden times the lion was considered to be the "king of beasts." Kings are supposed to be "proud, honorable and dignified." So, by stretched analogy, the accidental group of separate stars in Leo, millions of billions of miles away, was also imagined to be "proud, honorable and dignified." And that's why Quigley imagines she *knows* that the group of stars some ancient astrologer happened to call Leo would transmit pride, honor, and dignity to the president's ceremony.

What does Quigley mean by "Leo Ascendant." A planet or constellation that is near the eastern horizon and therefore beginning to rise in the morning sky is ascending, therefore "in the Ascendant." By stretched analogy, if a planet or constellation is rising it is getting more powerful. So "Leo Ascendant" gives the president's ceremony more of its qualities of pride, honor, and dignity.

Quigley did some astrological "cardstacking" here. A lion can be very vicious when killing and eating an innocent lamb, but Quigley decided to ignore that violent aspect of the stretched analogy to lions. She chose to imagine that gentle Leo gave only his good qualities to the Bitberg ceremony.

Another astrologer might have chosen to see the lion as violent and warned the president not to have the ceremony at the dangerous time of 11:45 A.M. when Leo was "in the Ascendant."

Suppose ancient astrologers had imagined they saw a chicken in the sky for the constellation, instead of a lion, and therefore called it "Chickie," not Leo. In that case the constellation of Chickie might well be viewed by today's astrologers as influencing people and events to be more like chickens than lions—perhaps timid and cowardly rather than proud, honorable, and dignified.

ASTROLOGY IS BASED ON BELIEF IN ANCIENT GODS

The Romans, borrowing ideas from the Greeks of ancient times, imagined that the god Mars caused the planet Mars to move through the sky. Similarly, the god Jupiter was supposed to move the planet called Jupiter; the goddess Venus moved the planet Venus; the god Mercury moved the planet Mercury; and the god Saturn moved the planet Saturn.

The fact that ancient Roman astrologers used the same names for the gods as for the planets tells us that they thought of them as almost the same. For that reason it seemed reasonable to them to look for clues as to what the gods might be like from the appearance of the planets they caused to move.

The planet Mars has a reddish appearance. That reminded ancient astrologers of blood, which reminded them of violence and war. Wars were fought by strong, brave men who hoped for victory. So, by stretched analogy, ancient astrologers imagined that Mars was the god in charge of war, violence, courage, manliness, soldiers, and victory—and any similar qualities they could imagine.

That's where Quigley got her idea that "Mars in the 10th [house] showed a kind of victory." This reasoning tells us that she accepts as true the ancient Roman superstition that the god-planet called Mars controls human wars, bloodshed, violence, victory, and similar qualities of human life and events.

Another astrologer could just as well have chosen the influence of Mars on the ceremony at Bitberg to mean violence. That would have matched the violent side of Leo, the lion. Such an astrologer could have come to an opposite conclusion from Quigley, that 11:45 A.M. should be avoided because it predicted violence.

The planet Jupiter moves much more slowly across the sky than Mars or Venus. By stretched analogy, astrologers of old probably imagined Jupiter to be older, therefore the chief god. He was thought to be more mature, wiser, and beneficial. That's why astrologer Quigley says that Jupiter is the planet of "benevolence and good will" and "represented the public."

The planet Venus looks beautiful in the sky, so ancient astrologers imagined it to be a female god whose influence on people would be about beauty, love, and womanly matters.

We now know that Mercury is the planet closest to the sun. For that reason it appears to move more rapidly in the sky than any other planet. To ancient astrologers this faster motion provided the clue that Mercury, the god, was young and speedy. That is why Mercury, the god, is often pictured as having winged feet, serving as the messenger for the other gods. (Figure 4.3)

By stretched analogy, Mercury's fast motion in the sky led ancient astrologers to put him in charge of human transportation, communication, business, and commerce. Today's astrologers do the same.

Saturn is the slowest-moving visible planet so it was thought to be the "bringer of old age" and "cold." These qualities reminded astrologers of approaching death, so Saturn's influence on earthly things was often considered to be more harmful than beneficial.

All this supernatural magic by ancient gods is an example of fairy-tale thinking. It has little to do with anything we observe in the real world. But that is the way astrologers of today think. What is the chance that any forecasts they make, based on these ideas, would be true?

With such fairy-tale thinking and extremely stretched analogies it is clear that *astrologers really do not know what a fact is!* They seem to believe that whatever they choose to imagine to be true is really so.

Figure 4.3. Ancient astrologers pictured their god Mercury with magical winged feet, serving the gods as a messenger. This remains today as a modern symbol for speedy delivery. Today's astrologers still follow this ancient superstition when they assume that the role of Mercury (the god), as a speedy messenger, causes Mercury (the planet) to "influence" transportation and commerce on earth. (Courtesy of Florists' Transworld Delivery)

Why should anyone believe in the predictions astrologers make with such fairy-tale thinking?

WHY DO PEOPLE BELIEVE IN ASTROLOGY?

It is unfortunate that today's *astronomers,* scientists who study the sky, kept the ancient names for constellations and planets that were based on untrue myths. As a result, people who know very little about astronomy mistakenly think that the mythical names for constellations are "scientific." This makes astrology also seem "scientific."

Three new planets have been discovered during the past few centuries. Astronomers made a mistake by continuing to name them after ancient gods: Uranus, Neptune, and Pluto. Astrologers eagerly assigned mythical new powers to those new planet-gods just the way ancient astrologers did. In Quigley's book, here is how fairy-tale thinking leads her to assign astonishing effects on human affairs to these new planet-gods, without a single bit of evidence!

How baffled the early astrologers must have been when they could not account for the deceptions, rumors, and drug or alcohol abuse caused by Neptune, or the overnight success or sudden collapse of fortune so typical of Uranus. Neptune and Pluto together in the air in the sign of Gemini were responsible for the miracle of flight in the early 1900s, and Pluto rules, among other things, that uniquely 20th century phenomenon, the media.

According to such reasoning, why should we honor the Wright brothers for inventing the airplane when Neptune, Pluto, and Gemini really did it? Why blame drug dealers, liars, and rumor-mongers when Neptune really made them do it? And if something is wrong with the media—newspapers and television—why not blame it on Pluto?

Unfortunately, the more than 1,000 newspapers that publish those daily, meaningless horoscopes do not tell their readers that it is all based on ancient superstition and fairy-tale thinking. Many people, especially children, believe practically everything they read. So why should we be surprised that so many people believe in the ancient superstition of astrology?

*   *   *

In Part One of this book we investigated the nature of superstition. We showed that it is based on fairy-tale thinking that ignores facts.

In the remaining chapters of this book—Part Two—we examine the powerful scientific way of thinking that enables us to obtain facts about the world and has greatly increased our knowledge and ability to do things.

Along with the many good things this scientific knowledge has brought to the world, it has also produced some harmful effects. As a result, a major task today is for people everywhere to learn how to use this powerful way of thinking to solve the many problems that now confront the world.

We begin, in chapter 5, with some answers to the important question, "How are new facts discovered?"

PART TWO

SCIENCE AS A WAY OF THINKING

5

How New Facts Are Discovered

There have always been some great thinkers who put facts ahead of superstitious, fairy-tale methods of thinking. We might call them the early "scientists." But it has been mainly in the past 500 years that the scientific way of thinking has been widely accepted. As a result, today we are able to discover important new facts about our environment very much faster than ever before.

In the chapters that follow you will see how the scientific way of thinking developed and how it has changed our world. But first, in this chapter, let's examine how the scientific way of thinking differs from superstition and fairy-tale thinking, and how we use it to build our knowledge.

AN EXAMPLE: CAN ROCKS FALL FROM OUTER SPACE?

Before the year 1803 the idea that rocks could fall from the sky seemed utterly ridiculous. Where would the rocks be coming from? Is someone sitting up in the clouds with a pile of rocks throwing them down on us? Impossible!

There had been occasional reports from distant places of rocks falling from the sky and hitting the ground with a loud crash. However, in 1803 there were no telephones, radios, cars, or airplanes, and it was hard to investigate sketchy reports from faraway places. So, there were no reports from trustworthy observers that rocks could actually fall from above. Such an

47

idea was considered to be just a product of imagination.

Then, on August 26, 1803, many people in the village of Laigle in France *saw* fast-moving bright streaks of light in the sky. They *heard* crashing sounds. Afterwards, they *found* many new crater-shaped pits of different sizes in the ground near the village. Each crater contained a rock that people could *see* was quite different from those usually found in the area.

Although it was hard to believe, the people of Laigle were quite sure of the fact that a shower of rocks had somehow fallen to earth.

People elsewhere were skeptical about these incredible reports. But reports from so many people in Laigle could not be ignored so easily. So a team of scientists went to Laigle to investigate. In a large area, six miles long and three miles wide, they *observed* about 3,000 new crater-shaped pits in the ground, each containing a strangely shaped rock. From such strong *evidence,* based on many observations, the scientists concluded that a shower of rocks, moving at high speed, really had fallen from above.

Where had they come from? The only explanation that made sense was that these rocks had fallen to earth from outer space.

A report by the scientists about their observations, with a proposed explanation of what happened, was published worldwide, in newspapers and science magazines.

At first, the idea that rocks could fall to earth from outer space was considered by many scientists to be a *hypothesis,* a reasonable guess for a possible fact, based on some evidence. Such a startling new hypothesis stimulated scientists to seriously consider the idea. Many of them began to look for further evidence for or against it.

HOW OUR KNOWLEDGE GREW

The discovery that rocks could fall to earth from above opened the door to a new area of knowledge in astronomy that grew very rapidly as many new observations were made. Today, the knowledge gathered since the event at Laigle in 1803 plays an important part in the picture scientists now have of the way the earth, sun, moon, planets, and all the stars were formed many billions of years ago.

All of this knowledge is based on careful *observations.*

For example, it was observed that before the rocks hit the ground, they were often seen by people hundreds of miles away, rapidly streaking across the entire sky as brightly glowing "fireballs." This observation showed that they were at a great height in the atmosphere and traveled at enormous speed.

Astronomers have *instruments* that enable them to *measure* the height above ground and speed of these fireballs. They are found to be traveling at speeds of about ten miles a second and begin to glow in the upper atmosphere at a height of about 50 miles.

Because of their resemblance in the sky to *meteors,* the falling rocks were called *meteorites.* We now know that the main difference between meteors and meteorites is their size. Meteors are very tiny; most are the size of grains of dust. When they hit the earth's atmosphere at enormous speed, friction with the air heats them and they glow for only a moment before the small amount of material is burned up or evaporates.

Meteors may be seen on any clear, moonless night, far from city lights, as quick streaks of light that usually last for only a second or so. The larger the grain of dust (perhaps the size of a grain of sand), the longer and brighter the streak.

Photography is one of the most important aids to astronomers because it captures observations at a moment in time. Figure 5.1 shows how useful photographs can be. This one, taken while the lens of the camera was kept open for several hours, captured the image of a meteor that happened to flash across the northern part of the sky during that time. As the earth rotated, the circular streaks were produced by bright stars as they appeared to revolve around the North Pole.

Note how the meteor streak widens and narrows at several places as parts of it burned, evaporated, or broke off because of the heat caused by friction with the air at high speed.

Some meteorites fell closely enough to where scientists lived so that they could be examined shortly after they fell to earth. It was observed that the outside of a newly fallen meteorite is very hot because of friction with the air. However, when broken open, the interior was found to be extremely cold because the meteorite had been in very cold outer space for a very long time.

Some meteorites in museums are enormous. The meteorite shown in Figure 5.2 is just one piece of a huge meteorite that produced the crater shown in Figure 5.3.

Figure 5.1. This photograph of the northern sky was taken with the lens open for several hours. The circular arcs show the apparent motion of northern stars as the earth rotated. The straight line streak is the track of a meteor that flashed across the sky while the lens was open. (Photo by W. Lockyer, Lockyer Observatory, England)

SOME GIGANTIC FALLS OF METEORITES

The biggest fall of meteorites since the one in Laigle occurred one morning in 1908 in a remote area of Siberia, in Russia. Many people saw an immense fireball streak across the sky, then heard distant thundering sounds that ended in a loud crash heard up to 650 miles away!

The impact was so powerful that people and horses 100 miles from the site of the crash were blown over by the wind, and some were knocked unconscious! Giant waves formed in rivers. In broad daylight, people living 250 miles from the crash saw a jet of flame about twelve miles high. Earthquake shocks were

Figure 5.2. The man's hand in this photograph indicates the large size of this meteorite. It is just one of many that had hit the earth at the same time and formed the huge crater in northern Arizona shown in Figure 5.3. Note the pock-marked surface caused by melting or breaking of outer parts of the rock as it hit the air at extremely high speed. (Courtesy of Meteor Crater Enterprises)

reported on measuring instruments all around the earth.

There were no cities or villages in the area where the rocks fell, so there were no known deaths. However, anyone who happened to be within many miles from the center of that crash would probably not have survived to tell about it.

The place where the meteorites fell was so remote that it was not observed by scientists until nineteen years later, and then only from an airplane. They saw a completely devastated area about 50 miles in diameter, with most of the trees knocked down, as though blown over by an incredibly powerful wind.

Two hundred craters were observed from the air. There surely are many thousands of smaller ones that were not visible from the airplane.

Whatever hit the earth was certainly a huge mass, perhaps as big as a large ship. The mass seems to have exploded into many pieces before reaching the ground. Such an explosion could have been caused by sudden heating and boiling of frozen gases. We now know that comets are composed of rock, ice, and frozen gases. One of the many comets in orbit around the sun may have hit the earth, causing the devastation in Siberia in 1908.

We do not know of anyone killed by meteorites, but there have been some close calls. In 1946, a hail of meteorites in Kenya, located in East Africa, flattened huts in many villages over an area sixty miles wide. One village was set afire and many cattle were killed. Fortunately, no people died in that incident.

METEORITES IN THE PAST

Can we figure out what happened in the distant past, even though no one ever observed the events? Yes, by using our marvelous brains and ability to reason logically. Like detectives, scientists search for clues to figure out what probably happened. We can *infer* (conclude from evidence) some details about events that probably happened in the past from what we observe in the present.

There is very strong evidence that some very large meteorites fell to earth in the distant past. We find a number of circular "impact craters" on earth, of many different sizes, up to many miles in diameter. One such crater, in Arizona, is shown in Figure 5.3. It is almost a mile in diameter and deeper than a 60-story building. Compare its size to that of the tiny road seen in the picture, taken from an airplane.

From magnetic measurements we know that a large mass of iron, often found in meteorites, lies beneath the crater floor. The evidence indicates that this crater was caused by the impact of a gigantic meteorite many years ago.

Geologists have several ways to estimate the ages of rocks. From their observations and measurements they estimate that this crater was formed about 12,000 years ago.

A number of other large impact craters have been discovered, often by noting large circular features on maps or photographs from satellites. Most of these were formed many millions of years ago, as shown by the way they have been eroded (worn away by rain, wind, rivers, and ice) over a long time.

Figure 5.3. Meteor Crater, almost a mile in diameter, was produced by the impact of a huge mass of rock about 12,000 years ago. The main mass buried itself underground, but many smaller meteorites are scattered around the site. (Arizona Office of Tourism)

METEORITES IN THE SOLAR SYSTEM

Other evidence about what happened in the distant past comes from observations with large telescopes of the surfaces of planets and their moons. Many "impact craters" are observed on our own moon (Figure 5.4), on Mercury (Figure 5.5), and on most moons revolving around the other planets. The way some of these craters overlap indicates that they occurred at different times.

Additional evidence for rocks in space came from discovery of many "small planets," called *asteroids,* that orbit the sun. They range in size from the largest, Ceres (pronounced as "series"), about 900 miles in diameter, down to some of irregular shape that are only about one mile long. There must be many more that are too small to be visible in our best telescopes.

More evidence for rocks in space, of many sizes, came from the spaceship Voyager II, which flew past Saturn in 1984. Scientists planned an experiment in which radio signals were transmitted to earth through Saturn's rings. (Figure 5.6) From observations of the way these radio signals were weakened astronomers were able to infer that they probably contain dust, rocks, and boulders of many sizes, all revolving in orbit around Saturn.

Other evidence about the nature of materials in space came from a space probe sent up from Russia in 1986 to investigate Halley's Comet as it approached the sun from far out in space, on its elongated 76-year orbit. Close-up pictures revealed that

Figure 5.4. The moon's surface reveals many thousands of craters, of many sizes, caused by impact of gigantic meteorites in the distant past. (Lick Observatory)

it was a peanut-shaped mass, about 8 miles long.

A bright halo of vapors and dust streamed outward from the head of the comet. This is what formed the bright tail which always points away from the sun. Scientists have found in the laboratory that light exerts slight pressure on objects it strikes. Out in space, that pressure of sunlight on a comet's dust and gases pushes them in a direction away from the sun.

Figure 5.7 shows the spectacular, bright "tail" of illuminated gases and dust from Halley's Comet as it appeared in 1910. It was an astonishing sight, stretching across one-sixth of the entire arc of the sky and estimated to be many millions of miles in length.

Astronomers concluded from these and other observations that comets are composed of a central mass of rock, or perhaps loose groups of rocks, mixed with ice, frozen gases, and dust.

The dust and gases released by comets, and perhaps small rocks that break free, wander off into orbit around the sun. Some of these materials eventually hit planets and moons,

Figure 5.5. This photograph, pieced together from a number of separate pictures taken by Mariner 10 as it passed by Mercury, shows many craters similar to those on the moon. (National Aeronautics and Space Administration)

perhaps our own earth. We then see them flash through the atmosphere as meteors, or reach the ground as meteorites.

It is also likely that some of the dust and rocks that hit the earth have been orbiting the sun from the very beginning of the solar system.

Scientists can identify many tiny bits of dust floating in the air as having come from meteors. They also find such particles in deep deposits of mud at the bottom of the ocean. This shows that the earth has been bombarded by a rain of dust particles from outer space for a very long time, probably from the beginning of the solar system.

From all this evidence it is clear that there are an enormous number of pieces of material in the solar system. There are planets, moons, asteroids, comets, boulders, and rocks of all sizes. There are huge numbers of objects the size of grains of sand and particles of dust. There are also many separate atoms and molecules of different kinds of gases.

This does not mean that outer space is crowded. The volume of the solar system is so great that the chance of a rock, or even a sand-size particle, hitting one of our manned space-

Figure 5.6. Saturn's rings are composed of huge numbers of different sizes of dust, larger particles, rocks, and boulders, all orbiting the planet. (National Aeronautics and Space Administration)

ships is extremely small. At their very high speeds (many miles a second) the impact of a sand-size bit of material could damage a spaceship and lead to the death of the astronauts inside. Fortunately that has not yet happened, but it is always a danger.

On earth we are well protected from damage by our 50-mile thick atmosphere that stops all but the larger rocks that come from outer space.

EVER-GROWING KNOWLEDGE

What began as a startling observation of rocks falling from the sky near the town of Laigle in 1803 has led astronomers to a much deeper understanding of our earth and solar system. It has also provided important information about events that occurred billions of years ago.

Today, such information, based on observations, plays an important part in theories about how the solar system was formed about four and a half billion years ago. Astronomers have good evidence that the solar system began as a huge cloud

Figure 5.7. In 1910 Halley's comet produced this enormous tail of gases and dust more than a hundred million miles long. It stretched across one-sixth of the sky. When the comet returned in 1986, a space probe sent from earth revealed a peanut-shaped "head" composed of rock and frozen gases about 8 miles long. (Mount Wilson Observatories, Carnegie Institute of Washington)

of gas and dust in space that was pulled together by the force of gravity. Our own earth was probably formed in this way from the dust and rocks that fell into the growing mass. The knowledge gathered about meteors and meteorites since the fall of rocks in Laigle in 1803 is an important part of that evidence.

We see in the history of our knowledge about meteorites an example of the way science grows, fact by proven fact. Discovery of one new fact often leads to discovery of others. This accumulation of experience and knowledge enables many thousands of modern scientists to increase our ability to solve problems that constantly arise in our world.

This scientific way of thinking is widely applied in engineering, industry, and medicine. It is increasingly applied to economics and the social and political sciences.

Today we have entered an *information age* in which knowledge has become power. Those who know how to use the scientific way of thinking, and therefore know how to get new information and use it properly, are the ones who will create new inventions and solve the difficult problems of our time.

As we shall discuss in chapter 10, there have also been some harmful results of such use of knowledge. One of the big problems of our time is to find ways to use our knowledge wisely to create a better world. Perhaps *you* will play a role in this important task.

THE MAIN IDEAS IN SCIENTIFIC THINKING

1. Facts must be based on accurate, carefully *checked* observations, *verified* by many people. These are the main ideas in scientific thinking that make it so superior to the kind of fairy-tale thinking upon which superstition is based.

2. Scientists use *imagination,* as well as *logical reasoning* to build on the facts they have. They make *hypotheses*: reasonable guesses as to possible explanations for what we observe. But these hypotheses are not considered to be true until supported by very strong *evidence.*

3. *Experiments* are often designed to get new observations to test hypotheses.

4. Scientists are *open-minded* about new ideas, but also reasonably *skeptical* about accepting them as true too quickly. History is full of examples when people thought they were absolutely right about facts and theories that later were shown to be wrong.

*   *   *

The scientific way of thinking has meant much more to our society than just the gathering of facts about our environment. During the past 500 years it has deeply affected the way people think about many things, including the way their governments operate.

Science has played an important role in the establishment of democracy in our nation and in many others in the world. How that happened is discussed in the next chapter.

6

Science and Freedom of Thought

Get into your time machine and go back 2,000 years. Imagine that you are observing the sun in the sky with an astronomer of that time. At dawn you see the sun appear to rise in the eastern sky and then go higher and higher until noon. Then it seems to move lower and lower in the afternoon, setting in the west in the evening.

Your ancient astronomer friend says, "I've watched this happen for many years. From these observations it is clear that the sun always moves in the sky from east to west. Someone with enormous power must be making it move. Only a god could do that. We believe it is Apollo, the god in charge of the sun.

"Some people say that he pulls it with his magical chariot, but I really don't know about that. All I know is that he gets the job done. Since we are not gods, we will never know how Apollo does it. It's not a problem for me, so I don't lose any sleep over it."

This explanation upsets you because you learned in school that it is not true, so you say, "Excuse me for differing with you, but no god is pulling the sun. The sun only *seems* to rise and set. Actually, we live on a huge, round, ball-shaped earth that rotates on its axis once a day. The earth's rotation gives us the *illusion* that the sun is moving when it really is not. It's like being on a merry-go-round and seeing everything else go around us, when *we* are really rotating with the earth."

The astronomer stares at you for a moment and says, "A very clever theory. But you and I both *saw* the sun move up from the east in the morning. We *watched* it move across the sky all day, and then go down below the horizon in the evening. Are you doubting what you actually *see*?

"Besides, we know that the earth is enormous. The known part of the earth stretches for thousands of miles from here in every direction. If, as you say, it is rotating once a day, this means that its surface must be moving at enormous speed right now to complete that big turn. It might have to move a thousand miles an hour. We don't feel that impossible motion. So, your theory is obviously wrong."

This stumps you because you never thought about it before. Now that this enormous speed is brought to your attention, it does seem strange that you don't feel that thousand-mile-an-hour motion.

"Furthermore," he continues, "about this crazy idea of a round earth. See that lake over there. Can't you see that it is perfectly *flat*?

"Look. I'll make a diagram to show you." (Figure 6.1) "Here's some water in the ocean, at A. If the earth is round then all its water would flow downward, away from the top, and finally fall off the sides of the earth. It has to disappear somewhere, perhaps in Hades. But we don't see the water in the lakes and oceans moving that way. That proves your theory is wrong.

"And here is a man walking around the earth. When he gets to B he would be sliding downhill all the way, and probably also land in Hades.

"What about this poor man at the bottom of the earth, at C? How long could he hang on without also going to Hades?"

Your eyes light up triumphantly. "No. No. Gravity will pull everybody towards the center of the earth and also keep water, people, and everything else from falling off."

"Gravity? . . . Who is he? How does he do that?"

"Gravity is not a person," you reply. "Gravity is an invisible force that pulls everything down towards the center of the round earth."

The ancient astronomer replies, with a tone of voice as though he thinks you are pretty stupid. "How does this god, this Mr. Gravity, do this? Does it pull people with ropes? Do you see or feel any ropes pulling you down?

"Suppose I put a ten-foot-thick stone between me and the earth. Shouldn't that thick stone block whatever Mr. Gravity tries to do in pulling me down? Shouldn't I then feel lighter,

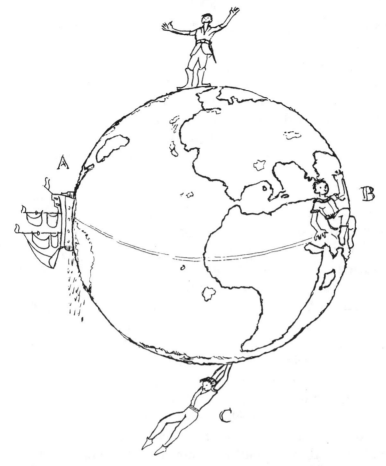

Figure 6.1. It was reasonable for people in olden times to think that a round earth is impossible. How could people, water, and ships keep from sliding off into Hades? It was very difficult to prove that an extremely mysterious "force of gravity" pulls everything toward the center of the earth. (Drawing by Albert Sarney)

maybe float in the air? You want me to believe that this pull, this gravity or whatever, passes right through solid rock without being stopped?"

At this point it dawns on you that you really do not fully understand this peculiar theory about the force of gravity in a round, rotating earth, something you were taught in school. You accepted this idea at school without thinking deeply about it. This reminds you of the way young children accept the story of Santa Claus without being puzzled by any of its contradictions.

Your talk with the ancient astronomer makes you realize that people in olden times were not so stupid when they thought the earth was flat and did not move. You also begin to understand that if you had lived long ago you, too, would have considered anyone a bit crazy to insist that what you see and feel is really not so.

In olden times, when there were no airplanes or satellites that go around the world, it was very difficult to prove that the earth is round and moves around the sun. That's why it took so long to discover the true nature of the solar system, and centuries more until most people were convinced it was true.

Today it is easy to prove that the earth is shaped like a ball. Just look at the photograph of our round earth, on the front cover of this book, taken from a satellite far out in space. Many airplanes have traveled around the world by constantly heading west, or east. If we make a telephone call at noon to India, on the opposite side of the earth, we find that it is midnight there. Such observations *prove* that the earth is round.

By far the best evidence that the earth and planets revolve around the sun comes from the amazingly accurate predictions astronomers now make about events involving the sun and planets. They measure orbits of the earth, moon, and planets with great precision, then predict, years in advance, exactly when and where eclipses will occur, and how long they will last. These predictions are accurate to a fraction of a second.

We have sent spaceships to the moon and many planets on journeys that could not have been made without precise calculations that take into account the forces of gravity of the sun, earth, moon, and planets. For example, in 1977, scientists sent Voyager II on a twelve-year journey to fly past the planets Jupiter, Saturn, Uranus, and Neptune, all hundreds of *millions* of miles away. Voyager II passed near each planet on schedule and reached Neptune, the last planet on its trip, within four minutes of the time planned by scientists twelve years before!

This is extremely strong evidence that our facts and theories about gravity and motion are true.

THE DANGEROUS IDEA OF A MOVING EARTH

In 1492 Columbus sailed to America and found a new continent. His ships did not fall over the edge of a flat earth, as many had feared. This fact cast doubt on the old theory of a flat earth.

Then Magellan sailed completely around the earth by heading mostly west. The fact that sailing mainly in one direction brings a ship back to its starting place was strong evidence, based on observations, that the earth is round.

When the Polish scientist Nicholas Copernicus proposed the theory that the earth revolves around the sun, this idea was much more difficult to prove, and even harder to accept.

It was also more dangerous for scientists to declare that they believed it true because the idea of a non-moving earth had become an important part of religious belief in Europe. People firmly believed that God had created the earth as the *center* of the universe, just for the benefit of people.

The Copernican theory shifted the center of the solar system to the sun. The other planets became equals with the earth because all of them revolve in orbits around the most-important sun. The earth was no longer the center of the universe.

Copernicus knew that his theory contradicted religious belief of that time and that to publish it would be considered *heresy*, the crime of differing in religious beliefs, punishable by burning at the stake. For that reason he delayed publication of his book until after his death in 1543.

However, some scholars read the book, became interested in his theory, and began to discuss it. Religious leaders of that time acted to suppress such discussion. In 1593 Giordano Bruno was imprisoned because he wrote books that favored the Copernican theory. He was found guilty of heresy by judges of the dreaded "Inquisition" and, in 1600, was executed by burning at the stake.

One of Bruno's "dangerous" ideas was that the stars were not on a fixed dome that revolved around the earth, as was believed at the time. He suggested that the stars are separate, bright objects, extending far off in space in every direction. Today we know this idea is also true. So Bruno was executed for having correct ideas.

Bruno's execution discouraged discussion by others and made them more cautious. But it did not stop scientists from continuing their observations of the skies.

In 1609, nine years after Bruno was executed, the Italian scientist Galileo Galilei heard about a Dutch invention of a telescope. He quickly put together some lenses to make one of his own and used it to observe the sun, moon, planets, and stars in the sky. By greatly magnifying the images of the sun, moon, planets, and stars, the telescope made details visible that no one had ever been able to see. This opened up the view of an astonishing universe that no one at the time could even have imagined.

WHAT GALILEO'S TELESCOPE REVEALED

For the first time people could see that those smudgy markings on the moon were really mountains, valleys, flat plains, and huge craters. Galileo was even able to estimate the heights of the mountains from their shadows. People could observe that the surface of the moon was similar to that of the earth.

Galileo's telescope also revealed dark spots on the sun that slowly moved around it, day after day. (Figure 6.2) If a huge body like the sun could rotate on an axis, why couldn't the earth also do so, as Copernicus claimed?

Galileo was surprised to see that the planet Venus often appeared with a crescent shape. (Figure 6.3) This shape is seen only if a moon or planet is closer to the sun than the earth. Only then do we see that most of its circular shape is dark. We then see only the narrow illuminated portion as a crescent. This observation confirms the prediction by Copernicus that

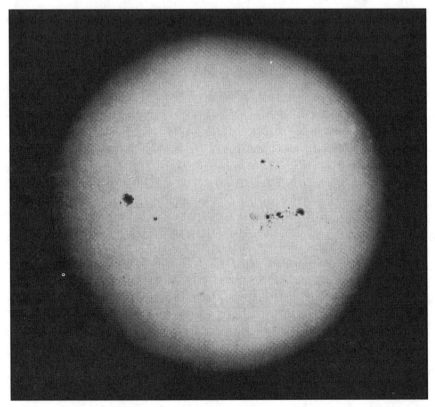

Figure 6.2. Galileo observed "sunspots" that moved from day to day, revealing that the sun rotated on an axis. If the sun rotated, why not the earth? (U.S. Naval Observatory)

Figure 6.3. We can only see the dark, night side of a planet if it is somewhat in front of us, off to one side of the sun. So, the crescent shape of Venus shows that it is closer to the sun than the earth, as predicted by Copernicus. (Mount Wilson and Palomar Observatory)

Figure 6.4. Note the four small moons of Jupiter (two in the upper left corner of this photograph, and two in the lower right corner.) They line up closely with Jupiter's equator, marked by the bands of clouds that encircle it. This system of moons greatly resembles a small solar system. (Lick Observatory, University of California at Santa Cruz)

the orbit of Venus is closer to the sun than that of the earth.

Galileo observed the planet Jupiter as a disk. There also seemed to be four small "stars" nearby, all in an approximately straight line with the planet. (Figure 6.4)

To Galileo's great surprise, the next night those four little "stars" had all changed position. This was an astonishing observation for that time because no stars had ever before been observed to move from their positions in the sky, which people imagined to be a fixed dome. Yet here were "stars" moving.

Night after night Galileo drew careful diagrams of the changing positions of these little "stars." It soon became clear to him that he was observing moons revolving around Jupiter! He measured the time it took for each moon to complete a revolution around Jupiter. As with the planets revolving around the sun, the moons farthest from Jupiter moved most slowly and took the longest time to complete one revolution.

For many people that was the most convincing evidence for the Copernican theory. They could observe in Jupiter a smaller model of the solar system, with its moons actually revolving

Figure 6.5. This telescopic view of a small section of the Milky Way reveals many details not observed with the unaided eye, especially the vast numbers of stars. Do you see any evidence for dark clouds in space? (Yerkes Observatory, University of Chicago)

around the planet, just as planets revolve around the sun.

Galileo's telescope also revealed about ten times as many stars as seen with the unaided eye. He observed the Milky Way to be far more crowded with stars than other parts of the sky. (Figure 6.5) This observation was strong evidence for Bruno's idea that the stars were not just attached to a dome around the earth, but were a vast number of separate stars, extending very far out into space.

Old ideas in *closed minds* die hard. The religious authorities of that time refused to accept this powerful evidence that proved them wrong. They ordered Galileo to stop writing and speaking in favor of the ideas of Copernicus and Bruno.

Galileo waited many years, but then, in 1632, he published a book about theories of the solar system. To avoid punishment for heresy he tried to disguise his views by writing the book as a "dialogue" between two people, for and against the Copernican theory.

No one was fooled. The arguments for the earth revolving around the sun were so much more convincing than for a non-moving earth that everybody could tell that Galileo really believed in the Copernican theory.

As happened with Bruno, Galileo was brought to trial for

heresy. The judges of the Inquisition found him guilty and he was imprisoned for the rest of his life. He was probably saved from execution only by his great fame as a scientist.

Galileo was *open-minded* and drew logical conclusions from facts that he actually observed. Facts based on observations meant little or nothing to the judges of the Inquisition. To them it was most important to stop anyone from spreading any ideas that challenged what the authorities believed to be true. They imagined that if a fact contradicted their beliefs then the fact had to be wrong! They really had no notion of what a scientific fact is.

This persecution of Galileo did not stop his ideas from rapidly spreading throughout the world. With the aid of Galileo's remarkable new instrument, the telescope, scientists in many countries kept gathering observations and drawing conclusions. In time, the ever-increasing evidence for a Copernican solar system established it as today's proven fact.

Many old ideas are true, so it is important that they be taught to young people and learned by them. But the big lesson from the persecution of Bruno and Galileo for their new ideas is that *some* old ideas may be wrong.

When new, observed facts are discovered that contradict the old ideas, we must view them with *open minds*. We have to seek more evidence until a proper judgment can be made as to whether or not the new ideas are true.

USING INSTRUMENTS TO HELP GATHER FACTS

In 1609 Galileo's telescope was one of the first of many modern instruments that have made today's world possible. It greatly enlarged our view of the universe and our place in it.

Modern telescopes, far more powerful than the one used by Galileo, enable us to observe a fascinating variety of objects in the distant universe. We know now that there are hundreds of billions of galaxies, each with many billions of stars. (Figure 6.6).

There are gigantic clouds of gas and dust in space. Increasing evidence shows that new stars are forming in some of these clouds. With the aid of a color-measuring instrument called a "spectroscope" we can analyze what is happening in stars that exploded long ago, hurling gases into space. (Figure 6.7) We

Figure 6.6. Modern telescopes reveal billions of very distant galaxies of many shapes and sizes. This spiral-shaped galaxy contains more than 100 billion stars. (Mount Palomar Observatory, California Institute of Technology)

can even show that the universe is expanding and probably began with a "Big Bang" about 15 to 20 billion years ago.

The development of photography during the past century has been extremely useful in science because it permanently captures images of what we observe at a moment in time. Then scientists can carefully study those observations, long afterward.

At the same time that Galileo made a telescope from two lenses, he also put them together in a different way to make a microscope. Although he did not do much with this new instrument, it was used by others to peer into the world of small things.

This new instrument also led to the discovery of remarkable new information, mainly in biology. Scientists soon discovered that tiny cells were the building blocks for all life. They observed such cells in every part of plants and animals, each doing a different job to make the entire organism work properly.

Scientists also discovered tiny one-celled plants and animals. It took another two centuries for them to show that some kinds of these tiny organisms could cause deadly diseases. From such discoveries we learned how to control many diseases and

Figure 6.7. Astronomers have evidence that this "nebula" (cloud of gases and dust in space) was produced by the explosion of a star many thousands of years ago. (Mount Wilson and Palomar Observatories)

to double the average length of life.

Today an immense variety of new instruments enables us to accurately observe and measure many quantities, such as length, weight, mass, force, time, pressure, speed, electric current, magnetism, light, color, and much more. Instruments have made it possible to observe invisible radiation, such as x-rays, infrared and ultraviolet rays, and radio waves.

Such instruments provide today's scientists with an enormous body of factual knowledge, based on observations, that could not have been imagined in Galileo's time. Engineers have used this knowledge to create today's giant industries. Physicians use this knowledge to prevent and cure diseases, prolonging life.

Special measuring instruments are also important in aiding our senses to know what is going on inside complex machines. A car has just a few of these instruments on the dashboard. An airplane pilot may have many more that give him vital information about the temperature of each engine, the air pressure above the wing, the speed of the airplane, the direction in which he is heading, the amount of fuel, and lots more. He can tell instantly when something goes wrong in a remote part of the airplane, and can usually make adjustments to prevent accidents.

NEW WAYS OF THINKING

Besides the important facts of science and the many inventions it has made possible, science has also given us a better way of thinking.

The sacrifices that Bruno, Galileo, and many others made to break through the brutal, closed-minded thought-control of the Inquisition were not in vain. They showed the world that authorities in power can be very wrong in what they insist are facts.

Science has also helped to diminish ignorance. We noted what terrible things ignorance could do in the Salem witch trials when the minds of people were poisoned by superstition.

Our Founding Fathers learned these lessons well when they created our Constitution and wrote the Bill of Rights in 1789. They put into the basic law of our land the ideas of freedom of thought, speech and religion, and democratic rights. These ideas have become an ideal for most of the world.

Freedom of thought does not guarantee that everyone will know what is true or false. Every person has the right to hold opinions and to make them known to others without being punished by authorities. But then we also have the responsibility to try to find out what the facts really are. That is where the methods of science come into play. They give us important guidelines for finding out what is true and what is false.

*   *   *

The best way to learn about the scientific way of thinking is to actually *use* it. This need not require complicated, expensive equipment. For example, what can you learn from the simple act of tossing some coins to see if they come down heads or tails?

In the next two chapters you will see how some simple experiments with coin tosses can lead to very surprising results. They will help you to understand why we should expect very unusual events to happen to people. And such experiments have also led to the discovery of *facts* that are now the basis of our huge insurance industry.

7

Developing a Theory: Probability

One day, while playfully tossing a coin, you suddenly wonder if the chance of getting heads or tails really is 50-50. Are half the number of tosses really heads and half tails?

At this stage all you have is a simple *problem* that arises, as most real problems do, from some observations while tossing coins.

Posing that problem required some *imagination.* Your dog, Sparky, would never think of it. But we humans have this unusual ability to think deeply, to play with *ideas.*

Your powerful ability to *reason logically* now comes into play. You examine both sides of the coin. They appear to be much the same, except for the picture stamped on it. So your reasoning leads you to think it *equally likely* for the coin to come down heads or tails. You make the *hypothesis* (reasonable guess at a possible fact) that half the number of tosses should be heads and half tails.

This hypothesis is not yet a fact, but only a possible fact that must still be *tested.* Many hypotheses turn out to be wrong. So, consider your hypothesis to be just the *start* towards establishing a fact.

The main way of testing a hypothesis in science is with *experiments.* In the case of tossing a coin the experiment is much easier than for most situations in life. Just toss a coin a number of times and observe what happens. There seems to be nothing to it, but note what happens when you actually start tossing a coin.

Suppose you decide to start with 10 tosses. Your hypothesis

predicts that in 10 tosses you should get $1/2 \times 10$ tosses, or 5 cases of heads, and 5 tails. Is that true? The way to find out is to try it and *observe* the outcome for tossing a coin 10 times.

You do this, but are disappointed when only 3 heads and 7 tails are observed. You expected 5 of each. Does this mean your hypothesis is wrong? Not yet. It's too soon to give up.

Continue tossing the coin for another *trial* of 10 tosses. Suppose that this time you observe 6 heads and 4 tails. Now you have a problem. Which is it, 3 heads out of 10, or 6 out of 10?

Aha! A new idea pops into your fertile brain. Your mysterious *intuition* is at work producing fruitful new thoughts. Perhaps 10 or 20 tosses are too few to get good information about how often a coin comes down heads. So, you decide to combine the results of the two *trials*.

You now have a total of $10 + 10$, or 20 tosses. If your hypothesis is right you should get half to be heads, or 10. There were 3 heads for the first trial of 10 tosses and 6 for the second. That's 9 heads in 20 tosses, a bit better than getting 3 out of 10 when you expected 5. But it still is not exactly the 10 you expected.

Your new idea about increasing the number of tosses is really a new hypothesis: the greater the number of tosses of a coin, the more likely it is that you will get half to come down heads.

Your mind instantly grasps the idea that to test the hypothesis you should toss the coin many times. You decide to keep a careful record of your observations by counting heads and tails as they occur.

Something very interesting is happening. The new hypothesis, added to the first one, is the beginning of a *theory* about probability. Think of a theory as a set of rules that describe the way events occur in nature. You are on the way to developing a theory about just one small bit of nature: what happens when a coin is tossed.

Test the hypothesis by tossing a coin 50 times, then 100, perhaps 200 times. Does the probability of getting heads (or getting tails) equal one half?

This experiment has been done by many people and they have found that the greater the number of tosses, the greater the likelihood that the number of heads would be very close to one half. So we consider it a fact that the probability of getting heads is one half. This fact is based on observations.

THE VALUE OF THEORIES

As you do experiments and observe what happens, your imagination will cause new thoughts to pop into your head when you least expect them. Your first experiment with tossing one coin at a time is likely to grow and push its way into new kinds of observations.

Suddenly you wonder: What would happen if you tossed two coins at a time? Would both coins be heads half the time? One-third? One-fourth? Something else?

Why only two at a time? How about three at a time, or four, or ten, or twenty? How many times in 100 tosses would all coins come down heads, or tails, or half heads and half tails, or some other combination?

Most of the rest of this chapter describes a "Theory of Probability" that gives us a way to predict the *expected* results of tossing coins in different ways. But not only for tossing coins. It has been found to work for predicting expected numbers of accidents, fires, deaths, results of card games, motions of atoms and molecules, chemical reactions, nuclear explosions, opinion polls, and much more.

Knowledge about this theory is the basis for the huge insurance industry and is also essential to all sciences. So, as you experiment with coin tossing you will be learning about the important subject of *probability.*

So, why not continue doing those experiments with tossing coins on your own, as far as you can go, before reading the rest of this chapter to find out what others have discovered? You will then get an actual experience in developing a theory all by yourself. You will also see how theories in general are developed.

We have theories in the sciences of physics, chemistry, biology, astronomy, geology, and in the practical uses of science such as engineering, architecture, and medicine. We have them in economics, education, and politics and in every other area of knowledge.

There are theories about how the universe began, how the solar system was formed, how continents move, how living things change, and evolve over time, how wars are started, how peace may be achieved, how recessions begin, how to end them, how to educate children, and lots more.

Such theories are a major way for getting new knowledge

because their many different hypotheses require testing and experimenting, which lead to new hypotheses, testing, experiments, observing, and reasoning.

THE THEORY OF PROBABILITY

In science and mathematics the word *probability* is used to describe the likelihood that some chance event would occur. For example, if you observe that for 100 tosses of a coin 50 of them came down heads, then the observed probability would be simply 50 divided by 100, or 1/2, or 0.5.

If an insurance company finds that during one year in a certain town with 10,000 homes, there were 100 cases of roof damage from storms, then the observed probability of roof damage per year is 100 divided by 10,000, or 100/10,000, or one in a hundred, or 0.01. Most people would describe that probability as "one chance in a hundred."

Suppose you toss two coins at a time. Before reading further use your reasoning ability to predict the probability that *both* coins would come down heads at the same time. Make a hypothesis about what the probability should be. Try it before you read further.

The two coins fall *independently* of each other. As one is falling there is no way it can affect what happens to the other coin. This is the key to predicting what will happen when both coins are tossed.

The diagram in Figure 7.1 gives us a way to analyze what happens. Consider what happens to the "First Coin," as shown on the first line. There are only two possible outcomes: heads (H) or tails (T).

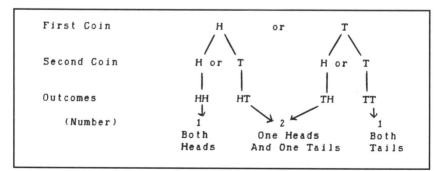

Figure 7.1. All possible outcomes for tossing two coins at one time.

The second line, marked "Second Coin," shows all the different ways the second coin could fall for each way the first coin can fall. So the line labeled "Outcomes" shows all the different ways two coins can fall heads or tails when tossed together.

Note the four possible outcomes: HH, HT, TH, and TT. Each of these outcomes is equally likely. Only one of these four gives us the "successful" outcome we seek: both coins heads (HH). So we can see that the probability that two heads will appear is one out of four, or 1/4, or 0.25.

In 100 tosses of two coins we would expect to see 1/4 × 100, or 25 cases when both coins are heads.

Try tossing two coins at a time for 100 times. Do you get exactly 25 cases of both coins coming down heads? Is this enough to confirm the hypothesis that the probability is 0.25?

How many times should you toss the two coins to get an exact answer?

A simple way to get many tosses is to have everyone in a class do the experiment. Then combine all the observations to get one total for the entire class. How close does your "observed probability" come to what is predicted from Figure 7.1?

The chart in Figure 7.1 gives us a way to predict the probability for any outcome when both coins are tossed. For example, what is the probability that both coins would come down tails? We note in Figure 7.1 that there is only one successful case in four when both coins come down tails (TT). So the probability is one divided by four, or 1/4, or 0.25.

This is the same probability as for getting both coins to come down heads. That makes sense because both sides of a coin are practically the same, except for the minor detail of the image stamped on it. So both coming down tails seems to be as likely as both being heads.

What is the probability of getting one heads and one tails? When we look at both coins after they have fallen, it doesn't matter to us which coin came down first and which came down second. Both cases appear to us to be "one H and one T." Figure 7.1 shows two such outcomes (HT and TH) in four tosses, so the probability is 2/4, or 1/2, or 0.5.

There is a quicker way to calculate that the probability of getting both heads is 1/4. Just *multiply the separate probabilities* (one-half) that each coin will come down heads. So, for two coins the probability for both being heads is 1/2 × 1/2, or 1/4, which is the same as obtained from Figure 7.1.

Why is this so? Only half of the tosses of the first coin will be heads, and we will get heads for both coins only if the second coin is also heads when the first coin is heads. So, the number of cases in which both coins are heads would be one-half of one-half, $1/2 \times 1/2$, or $1/4$.

All that is theory. But is it really true? The only way to find out is to test this prediction with an experiment. What do you find?

With this information you should be able to solve many problems about tossing more than two coins, on your own.

PROBABILITIES FOR TOSSING MANY COINS AT ONE TIME

Try these problems. When possible, test your answers with experiments to see if your predictions are correct. A discussion of each problem appears at the end of this chapter. Don't peek until you have first tried to find the answers yourself.

The chart in Figure 7.1 shows all the ways two coins can fall. You can make similar charts for the other questions, as needed.

1. Toss three coins together 100 times.

   a. How many times would you expect all three coins to be heads?

   b. How many times do you expect two heads and one tails? (Suggestion: make a chart for three coins like the one in Figure 7.1.)

2. When four coins are tossed together 100 times:

   a. How many times would you expect all four to be heads?

   b. How many times would you expect three heads and one tails?

   c. How many times would you expect the number of heads to equal the number of tails?

3. If you toss ten coins at one time, what is the probability of getting all ten heads? Are you likely to get one such outcome in 100 tosses of the ten coins?

FACTS AND THEORIES

In this chapter you have seen how new knowledge about chance and probability begins with *observations*. We *think* about what we observe and use our *imagination* and *intuition* to develop *hypotheses* that might explain what we see. Then we test those hypotheses with experiments. We reject any hypotheses which the experiments and observations show to be untrue and keep only those that are not contradicted by them.

This process leads us to new facts, new hypotheses, new experiments, and new tests with new observations. Soon we may have a *theory* that we think explains some events in the natural world.

In time, if we find that the theory continues to be applied without any contradiction by new observations, then the facts are considered *proved*. At that point we may refer to such facts as *principles* or *laws* of nature.

Facts, principles, and laws of nature are not absolute. In other words, we never consider them to be absolutely true. Some day a new observation, fact, or experiment may contradict a theory, principle, or law that we thought had been proved. When that happens, *the contradictory fact cannot be ignored.*

Sometimes a theory can be changed somewhat to explain or include the new fact. If that cannot be done, then the theory must be abandoned.

For example, Isaac Newton's Laws of Motion and Law of Gravitation held sway for several centuries. They were considered to be absolutely true because of great success in predicting eclipses with precision. Newton's Laws had even been used to predict where an unknown planet could be found in the sky. Astronomers found the new planet, Neptune, very close to the place in the sky where calculations had predicted it would be. After that remarkable feat most scientists thought Newton's Laws were absolutely true.

However, in 1887 an experiment by Albert Michelson and Edward Morley seemed to contradict Newton's Laws. The mystery was solved by Albert Einstein in 1905 with his Theory of Relativity. Einstein made a number of predictions to test his theory, all of which were found to be true.

Newton's Laws of Motion were not abandoned, but the method of calculation was changed somewhat to take into account Einstein's Theory of Relativity. Newton's Laws still work very well for most situations. But when objects or particles move at extremely high speeds (many miles per second), Newton's Laws have to take into account the changes Einstein described in the Theory of Relativity.

That is the way knowledge in science grows. It is also the way *all* knowledge must change to adjust to new facts. Increasing knowledge based on such scientific ways of thinking and doing has given us greater power to solve many kinds of problems. We have applied this knowledge in many ways to give us more control over the environment. We will also have to apply scientific thinking to solve many problems of our environment that modern inventions have produced.

In the next chapter you will see how the information about probability, described in this chapter, makes it possible for us to understand and explain some unusual, rather mysterious rare events that many people believe are caused by supernatural spirits.

You will see that it is unnecessary to assume a supernatural spirit as the cause for such events. You will also find out that some very unusual events are actually likely to happen.

DISCUSSION OF QUESTIONS

1a. *Probability of Three Tossed Coins Being All Heads.* From Figure 7.2 we see that the three coins come down all heads (HHH) for only one of eight possible outcomes. Therefore the probability of getting all three heads is one out of eight, or 1/8. For 100 tosses of three coins we expect to see $1/8 \times 100$, or 12.5 cases.

The probability could also have been calculated as:
$$1/2 \times 1/2 \times 1/2 = 1/8$$

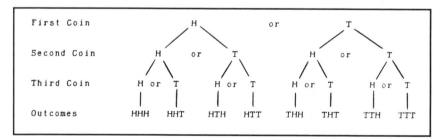

Figure 7.2. All possible outcomes for three coins tossed at one time.

The probability of each coin being heads is one-half. The second coin will be heads for only half of the cases when the first coin is heads. So for two coins the probability of both being heads is half of a half, or $1/2 \times 1/2$, or $1/4$.

The third coin will be heads for only half of the cases when the other two are both heads, or for $1/2$ of $1/4$, or $1/8$. This is the same as $1/2 \times 1/2 \times 1/2$.

You can see that as a coin is added to the group being tossed the probability of getting all heads is reduced by half. For four coins tossed at one time the probability that all come down heads is $1/2 \times 1/2 \times 1/2 \times 1/2$, or $1/16$.

1b. *How Many Cases of Two Heads and One Tail?* From Figure 7.2 we see three possible outcomes with two heads and one tail: HHT, HTH, and THH. So the probability is 3 out of 8, or 3/8.

2a. *Probability That Four Tossed Coins Would Be All Heads.* This has already been discussed in question 1a. The probability is $1/2 \times 1/2 \times 1/2 \times 1/2$, or $1/16$.

2b. *Three Heads and One Tail.* Make a chart for four coins tossed at one time. (Figure 7.3) You can observe four cases when there are three heads and one tail (HHHT, HHTH, HTHH, and THHH). From the chart you can count 16 possible ways that four coins could fall. Therefore the probability of getting three heads and one tail is 4/16, or 1/4.

2c. *Two Heads and Two Tails.* From Figure 7.3 you may observe six outcomes in which there are two heads and

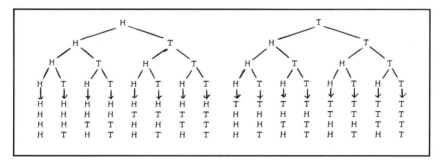

Figure 7.3. Outcomes for four coins tossed at one time.

two tails (HHTT, HTHT, HTTH, THHT, THTH, and TTHH). The total number of possible outcomes is 16. Therefore the probability of two heads and two tails is 6/16, or 3/8.

3. *Probability of All Heads When Ten Coins Are Tossed.* As explained in problem 1a, each additional coin in a group of coins that are tossed at one time reduces the probability of getting all heads by one-half. So for ten coins together the probability is 1/2 multiplied by itself ten times, or: $1/2 \times 1/2 \times 1/2 \times 1/2 \times 1/2 \times 1/2 \times 1/2 \times 1/2 \times 1/2 \times 1/2$, or 1/1,024.

This means that we are likely to observe only about one case of all ten heads in 1,024 tosses of ten coins. This is a rather rare event. Tossing them only 100 times, about one-tenth as many as a thousand, is not likely to produce even one case of all ten heads.

Can you calculate the probability of getting all heads when 20 coins are tossed at one time?

8

Unusual Events, Luck and Chance

Here is the story of an astonishing event that the author of this book (Mr. R) knows is true because it actually happened to him.

Mr. R dialed the telephone number of his friend Sam. After a few rings someone answered the phone.

"Is Sam there?"

"Yes. Just a minute. I'll call him."

Sam got on the phone and exchanged greetings with Mr. R, then asked, "How did you know I was here?"

"Why? Aren't you home?"

"No. I'm at my friend's house."

INCREDIBLE! Mr. R had dialed the wrong number and reached the person he wanted to talk to, *at that wrong number!*

This event is so unbelievable that many people assume it must have been caused in some supernatural way.

A SUPERNATURAL CAUSE?

An "explanation" based on supernatural magic raises more questions than it answers. Why would some supernatural being, or spirit, want to do this? The telephone call was of no special importance, nobody's life or health depended on it, and no money was involved. Did the supernatural spirit merely want to play a prank, perhaps have some fun by watching Mr. R's surprised expression when he realized what an unusual event had occurred?

There doesn't seem to be any *purpose* in having a mysterious supernatural spirit make the event happen.

Think about all the facts a supernatural spirit would have to know, and the many magical powers it must have, to *cause* this unusual call to happen.

1. The spirit would have to *want* Mr. R to dial a wrong number in just the right wrong way so the call would reach Sam away from home.

2. The spirit would have to be able to read Mr. R's mind and know, before the call, that Mr. R wanted to talk to his friend Sam on the telephone.

3. It would have to know that Sam would not be at home to receive the call.

4. It would also have to know that Sam would be in a friend's house at the very moment Mr. R made his call, or it would have to arrange for Sam to be there, which is even more miraculous.

5. The spirit would have to know the phone number of Sam's friend without looking in a telephone book.

6. It would have to get inside Mr. R's brain to direct his fingers to make the right mistakes to produce the wrong telephone call in the right way.

An "explanation" based on a supernatural spirit requires more unbelievable things to happen than the unusual event itself! Nothing in our experience, and nothing we can *observe*, gives us any *evidence* that anything could have the remarkable ability to make the electricity in the telephone wires go to the right place in the wrong way.

Some people might think they are explaining it when they say it happened because of "luck." This is another way of saying "by chance," but it does not explain how the unusual call might happen.

Scientists think in a different way. They want to know *why* things happen. There is a scientific explanation for what happened to Mr. R that is based on the theory of probability which you began to investigate in the previous chapter. To understand that explanation you need to know more about the fascinating nature of probability for events that occur by chance.

MANY KINDS OF CHANCE EVENTS

From experience with tossing coins you know that we cannot predict in advance whether a tossed coin will come down heads or tails. It is an unpredictable event that occurs by pure *chance.*

However, your experiments with tossing coins have also shown that we can predict approximately how many heads or tails to expect when a coin is tossed many times.

There are many other kinds of chance events, each of which has its own probability of occurrence. For example, if you pick any card from a full deck of 52 cards the probability of getting a spade is one-fourth because 13 of the 52 cards, or 13/52, or one-fourth, are spades.

Suppose you select a card from a full deck, and repeat this 40 times. You are likely to get a spade about 1/4 × 40, or 10 times.

Test that prediction with an experiment. But be sure to return the selected card each time one is taken from the deck, otherwise the pack from which you select would no longer have 52 cards. That would change the probability. Also, take cards from different parts of the deck. Do you get the number of spades you expected?

Suppose you now decide to look for aces. How many aces would you expect to get when you pick a card from a full deck and repeat this 100 times? There are four aces in the deck, so the probability of picking one from 52 cards is 4/52, or 1/13. You expect to get 1/13 × 100, or 7.7 (about 8) cards.

Try it. What do you observe?

The probabilities for many kinds of chance events are very small. For example, in the previous chapter one of the problems was to calculate the probability of getting all heads when 10 coins are tossed at one time. The answer, as described in the section at the end of chapter 7, was 1/2 multiplied by itself ten times, or 1/1,024. In other words, we expect to see only about one case of all ten heads for 1,024 tosses of ten coins.

An experiment to test this prediction would be very tedious. However, a computer could be programmed to simulate (imitate) the chance events for coin tosses, and could quickly run a test of many thousands.

Being hit by a meteorite is such a rare event that we do not know of anyone to whom this has happened. The probability is practically zero, but still, it might happen some day.

Being hit by lightning also has a tiny probability, but not as small as that for being hit by a meteorite. Yet it does happen occasionally.

Insurance companies keep careful records of many kinds of accidents. From this actual experience, based on observations, they can predict fairly accurately how many illnesses, deaths, car thefts, fires, car crashes, or home accidents are likely to occur each year. These figures can be used as "observed probabilities" to estimate how much should be charged for insurance to cover the cost of claims, plus profits.

In a similar way, Mr. R's unusual telephone call *could* happen, so there is a tiny probability that it might happen. We cannot tell who would make or get such a call, or when and where it would happen. However, we can estimate how likely it is to happen to someone in the world sometime in the future.

EXPLAINING THE UNUSUAL TELEPHONE CALL

Everyone occasionally makes a mistake when dialing or pressing the buttons for a telephone call. It makes a big difference if the mistake is made in the last four digits of a telephone number, or elsewhere in the number.

If the mistake is in the last four digits then *the call reaches a telephone in the same neighborhood as the person being called.*

Suppose you make a long distance call with a number like 123-456-7890. Dialing the first three digits (123) sends your call into a large city or region with several million people.

Dialing the second three digits (456) puts your call into a neighborhood in that city or county. Your call is now narrowed down to 10,000 people because the four remaining digits only allow for telephone numbers from 0000, 0001, 0002, 0003 . . . all the way up to 9999.

So, if Mr. R made a mistake in the last four digits he would reach one of 10,000 people in Sam's neighborhood.

We will have to make certain reasonable *assumptions* (facts assumed to be true) in order to make an estimate of probabilities. This is permissible so long as we do not forget that these are assumptions, not actual facts. We may do so because the probability we calculate will not be used for any practical purpose, but just to show that it is reasonable to expect Mr. R's kind of unusual call to happen to someone.

Assume that the probability of Mr. R making a mistake in the last four digits of a telephone call is 1/50. That is, he is likely to make such mistakes about once every 50 calls. This is a reasonable assumption because most people would make such mistakes more often than one call in 50.

A number of different, independent (not connected to each other) chance events must occur at the same time for Mr. R's unusual call to happen, as follows:

1. Mr. R dials Sam and makes a mistake in the last four digits. The probability is assumed to be 1/50.

2. Mr. R's call is now reaching one of 10,000 people in Sam's neighborhood. Most people will have some friends in the neighborhood whom they visit. Assume that Sam had 10 good friends in the neighborhood. In that case the probability that Mr. R's wrong call would reach a friend of Sam is 10 out of 10,000, or 10/10,000, or 1/1,000.

3. There is a certain small probability that Sam would happen to be at a friend's house at the very moment Mr. R's wrong call comes in. Assume that Sam visits these friends in the neighborhood for a reasonable 9 hours a year.

There are 24 × 365 hours in a year, or 8,760 hours. Since all of these calculations are approximate, it won't matter much if we round off the 8,760 hours to about 9,000. In that case the probability that Sam would happen to be at a friend's house, at the very moment Mr. R's wrong call comes in, is 9/9,000, or 1/1,000.

For Mr. R's wrong call to reach Sam, all of these independent chance events must occur together. How should we calculate the probability? Recall how this was done for tossing a number of separate coins. We just multiplied the probabilities of the separate events (separate coins falling.) For example, the probability of getting heads when three coins are tossed at the same time is 1/2 × 1/2 × 1/2, or 1/8.

So, the probability that Mr. R's call would occur is 1/50 (for making the mistake in the last four digits of the call) times 1/1,000 (probability that the call would reach a friend of Sam in the neighborhood) times 1/1,000 (probability that Sam would be at a friend's house when the call comes through.) Or:

1/50 × 1/1,000 × 1/1,000, or 1/50,000,000.

In other words we might expect this kind of unusual event to occur once in about every 50,000,000 (50 million) phone calls.

Whether or not such an unusual call is likely to happen to someone, sometime, somewhere in the world depends on how many calls are made. The exact number of calls in the world is not known. But an official of Nynex, one of the seven big telephone companies in the United States, has estimated that they handle about 100 million calls every day!

With 100 million calls every day, and a probability of one in 50 million for Mr. R's unusual call, you can see that we may expect such unusual calls to occur in the Nynex system.

There are 365 times as many calls in one year as in one day. There are also many other telephone companies throughout the world besides Nynex. Therefore, if our estimate of probability is correct, there ought to be a number of calls every year like the one Mr. R made. In other words, such an unusual call is *likely* to occur every year to someone, sometime, somewhere in the world! It may actually be happening to many people each year!

Of course, this assumes that the estimate of probability is correct. But even if the probability is really a hundred times smaller, that would not change our conclusion that the event would occur some time.

NO NEED FOR SUPERNATURAL MAGIC

Unusual events are bound to happen because something is constantly taking place, everywhere on our huge earth, every moment of every day, year after year. With five billion people around to observe them, it would be surprising if some very unusual things did not happen to some people.

Such an unusual event is likely to happen to you during your long lifetime. You cannot know in advance what kind of event it would be, or when and where it would occur. But if and when it does happen, you will understand how it could be a chance event, explainable by the theory of probability.

There is no need to assume that it was caused by some kind of supernatural spirit with magical powers.

OTHER KINDS OF UNUSUAL EVENTS

Here are two other examples of unusual events that actually happened. Use your reasoning power and knowledge of probability to explain how they could occur. Then read the "Discussion of Questions" at the end of this chapter.

1. *An Unusual Horse Race.* One day, people at a race track were startled to see an astonishing finish for one of the events that had seven horses. The horse with number 1 on its saddle came in first. Horse number 2 came in second. Horse number 3 came in third, and all the others ended up in "consecutive order": 1, 2, 3, 4, 5, 6, 7.

This is a very rare event because the outcome could have been any combination of seven numbers from 1 through 7, such as 3, 6, 2, 7, 5, 1, 4, or 6, 1, 7, 5, 2, 4, 3.

A photograph of this race appeared some time ago in a magazine, but is no longer available for this book. However, Figure 8.1 shows a similar, less rare outcome of a race in which the horse that came in first had the number 1 and the horse that came in second had the number 2.

Can you calculate the probability that the first two horses in a seven-horse race would cross the finish line in the order of 1, 2, as shown in Figure 8.1?

Can you calculate the probability that seven horses would cross the finish line in "consecutive order": 1, 2, 3, 4, 5, 6, 7?

Think about it, then see the "Discussion of Questions" at the end of this chapter.

2. *Winning a Big Lottery Twice.* Do you think it possible for someone to win a big, million-dollar lottery twice? That seems so unlikely as to be practically impossible. Yet it has actually happened to several people! (Figure 8.2)

Can you show that it is reasonable to expect such an unusual event to occur to someone, sometime?

Think about it, then see the "Discussion of Questions" at the end of this chapter.

In this book you have seen that explanations of events by supernatural magic are not necessary. You have also seen that scientific ways of thinking, based on observations, experiments, and logical reasoning give us great power to explain what hap-

Figure 8.1. In this unusual race with seven horses, horse #1 came in first and horse #2 came in second. Can you explain why we would expect this 1,2 outcome to occur about once in 42 races with seven horses? (New York Racing Association)

pens in our complicated world.

In the next chapter you will see how that power of scientific thinking has been used during the past few centuries to greatly increase our knowledge. It has changed the world in astonishing ways.

DISCUSSION OF QUESTIONS

1. *An unusual horse race.* As the horses keep crossing the finish line they leave fewer and fewer horses behind them, still running the race. For horse #1 in a seven-horse race the probability that it would come in first is one out of seven, or 1/7. For horse #2 (with six horses still in the race) the probability that it would come in second is 1/6.

The probability that both of these independent events would happen in the same race is therefore 1/7 × 1/6, or 1/42. We expect about one in 42 races with seven horses to end with a 1, 2 finish.

For the horses to come in 1, 2, 3, 4, 5, 6, 7, the probability is:

1/7 × 1/6 × 1/5 × 1/4 × 1/3 × 1/2 × 1/1, or 1/5,040.

We expect one in 5,040 seven-horse races to end with the

Figure 8.2. A woman once won a big lottery twice. This seems miraculous. Many people think it must have been arranged by supernatural means. Can you explain how such an extremely unlikely event might be expected to actually happen? (Drawing by Albert Sarney)

horses in consecutive order: 1, 2, 3, 4, 5, 6, 7.

There are many races per day, on many days of the year, on hundreds of racetracks throughout the world. If there are 1,000 races a year with seven horses, in 5 years there would be 5,000; in 10 years, 10,000. For such long periods of time it becomes quite likely that the one rare race in 5,040 would occur.

So we should expect it to happen some day. It already has.

2. *Winning the Lottery Twice.* Assume that, on the average, a million people buy tickets for each big lottery. Then the probability that any one person's ticket would be selected as the winner is one in a million, or 1/1,000,000. This is so small that it is extremely unlikely for any one particular person to win.

However, most lotteries are conducted every week or month in many countries on earth. Over the years there have been many lottery winners, perhaps a few thousand by now.

One woman who actually won twice, and had lots of money after she won the first lottery, bought 20 lottery tickets every week, trying to win again. In a year she had bought more than 1,000 tickets. In this way she increased her chances of winning again by about 1,000 times.

There are many new lottery winners each year, so their number keeps increasing. By now there probably are more than a thousand of them in the world. Some of them are probably also buying many tickets.

You can see that it is only a matter of time for one of the thousand or more winners to win again with one of their thousand or so tickets. So we may expect someone, somewhere in the world, sometime, to win a lottery twice.

9

Science Gives Us Real Knowledge

Get into your time machine and go back to the year 1540 to visit Nicholas Copernicus in Poland. You find him working on his theory that the earth revolves around the sun in an orbit. You tell him the following astonishing story:

In the year 1968 three men, called astronauts, entered an enormous tube-shaped vehicle as tall as a cathedral. Suddenly, an immense flame shot out from the bottom of the machine and continued to burn. The vehicle slowly rose into the air, moving faster and faster, higher and higher. (Figure 9.1)

Soon it was 100 miles up, out of the earth's atmosphere, in cold outer space. When the flame stopped, a large section of the spacecraft separated and wandered off. A smaller section, with the three astronauts, coasted toward the moon 240,000 miles away at a speed of more than 20,000 miles an hour!

The astronauts never felt that speed. In fact, they were able to float calmly in the air of the cabin. To move forward in any direction they merely pushed backwards against any surface.

Several days later, as they approached the moon, a flame at one end of the spacecraft was turned on, hot gases shot out and the astronauts maneuvered to go into orbit. The spacecraft continued moving, but now around and around the moon, like a planet moving in its orbit around the sun.

These precise maneuvers were timed by means of measurements with very accurate instruments and with complicated calculations made by computers that solve mathematical problems thousands of times faster than any human.

Figure 9.1. Apollo 11 carried three astronauts to the moon, and brought them back safely. Two of them actually landed on the moon. This was the first of several such trips, made possible by ever-increasing scientific knowledge. (National Aeronautics and Space Administration)

Two of the astronauts entered a small "lunar lander" that was released and slowly separated from the main spacecraft. (Figure 9.2) Then they turned on a flame at one end of the lander and used it to maneuver to a gentle landing on the moon.

The astronauts got into bulky, enclosed suits, each with its own air supply. Very heavy weights had been built into the shoes because the force of gravity is only one-sixth as much on the moon as on earth. Without those weights strongly hold-

Figure 9.2. This photograph shows the "lunar lander" with two astronauts aboard, just after its release from Apollo 11. Our beautiful earth appears as a large half-moon, just above the horizon. (National Aeronautics and Space Administration)

ing the astronauts down to the moon, every normal step they took would have caused them to jump dangerously high.

On earth, 240,000 miles away, hundreds of millions of people, watching television sets at home, saw the astronauts walking about on the moon. (Figure 9.3) They heard the astronauts describe this strange new world, and even saw what our beautiful, round earth looks like from the moon.

The astronauts spent several days exploring the area, taking pictures, doing experiments, and gathering rocks.

They began the trip back to earth by turning on the flame of the lunar lander to lift off from the moon. Then they maneuvered it to rejoin the main spacecraft, still moving in orbit. Once safely aboard, a flame at the back of the spacecraft was turned on to move it out of orbit around the moon and then head back to earth at high speed.

Eight days after it had left the earth the spacecraft approached the earth and was maneuvered into an orbit. The three astronauts entered a cone-shaped container that was then ejected from the main spacecraft. It entered the thin upper atmosphere at a glancing angle, more than 50 miles from the Pacific Ocean

Figure 9.3. Astronaut Aldrin sets up an experiment on the moon. Note the bulky suit, needed to maintain air supply and proper temperature on the airless, cold moon. (National Aeronautics and Space Administration)

below, at the enormous speed of about five miles a second.

It was more than a hundred miles from where it was to come down in the ocean. However, air resistance gradually slowed the container until a large parachute could be safely opened to slow the fall still more. Then it splashed safely into the vast ocean, bobbed to the surface and floated upright in the water.

A helicopter from a big ship that had been waiting nearby quickly flew to the astronauts, hovered above it, and dropped a rubber boat into the water.

The astronauts put on special garments to prevent new kinds of germs from being brought back from the moon, then got into the rubber boat. (Figure 9.4) One by one, the astronauts were lifted into the helicopter and flown to the ship.

They were immediately taken to a special room and remained there for 21 days while scientists made sure that they had not been contaminated by dangerous germs. After all, this was the first time people had been on the moon. No one could

Figure 9.4. After parachuting into the ocean in a special container, the three astronauts (Neil A. Armstrong, Michael Collins, and Edwin E. Aldrin, Jr.) put on airtight garments to be sure no harmful germs were brought back to earth. (National Aeronautics and Space Administration)

be sure there were no new kinds of germs on the moon, so precautions had to be taken. The three astronauts were hailed as heroes for the first visit to the moon by humans.

Copernicus would probably have thought your true description of these actual events to be a "fairy tale." He would have considered the following facts either impossible or incredible:

- Rocket motors produce enormous flames and forces that can propel spaceships carrying people to the moon, 240,000 miles away, and then return them to earth safely.

- Astronauts in space suits can safely walk on the moon where there is no air.

- Television enables millions of people to see and hear events on the moon, 240,000 miles away.

- Computers rapidly solve very complicated mathematical problems that no human could do, with astonishing speed.

- People can travel at speeds of thousands of miles an hour without feeling any motion.

- People float in midair in a spaceship when the rocket motor is shut off.

- On the moon we weigh one-sixth as much as on earth.

- Cameras can take pictures that show details far more exactly than the best artists can draw.

- People in a closed container can safely fall to earth from outer space by using a parachute.

- We are able to accurately calculate in advance where astronauts returning from outer space would parachute to earth.

- A ship can navigate so accurately that it can find its planned place in mid-ocean near where the astronauts are expected to fall to earth.

- We have flying machines called helicopters that can take off from a ship, carry a rubber boat for three men in the ocean, hover in midair, pick up the men, then safely bring them back to a ship.

- Tiny creatures called 'germs', so small they cannot be seen with the unaided eye, can cause disease.

You would have had great difficulty answering the many questions Copernicus might have asked. If he believed you, he would surely have wondered, "How did people learn to make spaceships that could take people to the moon and bring them back safely? How did they learn to do all that in only 430 years?"

"STANDING ON THE SHOULDERS OF GIANTS"

Space flight, as well as our modern way of life, would not have been possible without the knowledge we have obtained from many discoveries by thousands of scientists.

Consider the great contribution made by just one scientist, Isaac Newton. By 1687 he had worked out his Laws of Motion, Law of Gravitation, and a special kind of mathematics called "calculus." No space flight could be made today without using his discoveries about forces, motions, and how they may be calculated.

This knowledge enables space scientists to compute with great accuracy the forces and motions produced by rocket motors, the effects of gravity on the earth and moon, and the speed and direction of motion needed for spaceships to go into orbit or reach the moon.

For that matter, no large bridge, tall building, spaceship, car, airplane, radio, or television set could have been designed, built, or produced without knowledge of Newton's laws and calculus.

Newton thought of himself as "standing on the shoulders of giants." It was possible for him to make new discoveries about motion only because of the knowledge he obtained from earlier scientists like Galileo and others who had investigated the way objects fall.

Johannes Kepler was another scientific "giant" who had shown that the orbits of planets are not perfect circles, but oval shapes called "ellipses." This idea, too, played an important part in Newton's discoveries.

Copernicus had contributed the modern idea of our solar system with planets in orbit around the sun. Newton needed to know this to work out his laws of motion and of gravitation.

Further back in time there were many astronomers who gave us important knowledge about the sun, moon, and planets. Copernicus, Kepler, and Newton could not have made their discoveries without that information.

Many people who were not scientists also contributed to modern space flight. Johannes Gutenberg invented a method of printing that made it possible to produce the books that gave Newton the knowledge he needed to make his discoveries. Others, much further back in time, had invented writing, reading, pen, ink, and paper.

Still others invented machines and materials of many kinds that made it possible to produce spacecraft, instruments, and computers without which trips to the moon would have been impossible.

Everybody needs food and shelter to stay alive. So scientists and inventors could not have done their work without the many people, past and present, who found new ways to grow and harvest crops, breed new varieties of plants and animals, transport food, build houses, or make clothing. All contributed, not only to space flight, but to building our civilization.

Modern civilization would not be possible without schools to transmit the knowledge of the past to our young people. What took a great scientist years to discover is often quickly taught and learned by today's students. Most of the factual knowledge in any modern science textbook would have astonished Copernicus, Galileo, and Newton. Yet many students take that wealth of precious knowledge for granted.

Such knowledge does not make young people great scientists. But what they learn today does give them the opportunity to"stand on the shoulders of giants" and make their own contributions to knowledge some day.

All of us stand on the shoulders of giants. Every bit of food we eat, the clothes we wear, the houses we live in, and anything else we know how to make or do today would not be possible without the knowledge given to us by people who lived in the past. We must be ever grateful to the many thousands of people, past and present, who made it all possible.

What part of these great accomplishments has been contributed by the superstitious way of thinking? Absolutely nothing. The belief in fairy-tale magic has blocked attempts to explain how and why things happen. Today it is a lazy person's excuse to avoid thinking about *why* things happen.

Not until many of us learned how to use scientific ways of thinking was it possible to greatly improve everyday life, as well as go to the moon.

Unfortunately, we have not yet learned how to fully use our knowledge properly. Wars can now be far more destructive than before. Too many people in the world still starve to death. Pollution is increasing and the environment is being severely damaged.

Scientific ways of thinking can help solve many of today's problems. The next chapter discusses some of these problems and suggests ways they may be solved.

10

Science: Past, Present, and Future

The next time you meet with your class at school think about this: If your classmates had been living around the year 1500, about one-third of them would not have survived their first decade of life. Most people died before the age of thirty, mainly of diseases that are easily prevented or cured today.

THE PAST

In those days physicians knew practically nothing about what caused most diseases. They had very few medicines that worked. None were available to ease severe pain. They could not repair broken bones properly. To save lives they often amputated arms and legs, without anesthetics. People knew nothing at all about germs, viruses, vitamins, or minerals.

Physicians did not know that the blood is circulated through the body by the pumping action of the heart. They were not even aware that washing hands was important in preventing disease.

Farming was very difficult because there were no tractors to plow the earth or harvest crops. There were no trucks or trains to bring food to people in distant cities. Most people had to be farmers because families could produce only slightly more than enough food for their own needs.

Horses or oxen were used for some jobs, but most hard physical work had to be done by human labor. There were simple devices for producing some kinds of goods by hand, but this required a lot of time and effort. People often had to sew their own clothing and even make their own thread and cloth. To survive they usually had to work from sunrise to sunset.

Most young children had to work hard to help provide food and shelter for the family. Schools or tutors were available only for the wealthy. Most people never learned to read and write.

Books, magazines, and newspapers were not readily available because printing was not invented until 1447. Before that time books had to be handwritten, word by word, page by page. As a result, people knew very little about the world beyond their own towns.

Most people never traveled more than a few miles from where they were born because walking was the only way they could go anywhere. Only a few of the wealthy could afford horses or ride in bumpy, horse-drawn carriages, often on unpaved, muddy roads.

There were no telephones, so communication with other areas was difficult and slow. Even sending or receiving a letter was a problem because few people could read or write. Letters had to be carried by men on horseback or in horse-drawn carriages.

So, when anyone talks about the "good old days" don't be misled. Life was very difficult for most people, and their lives were usually short. Kings and queens of old would have envied the way most people live in our country today.

Then, after about 1500, came the modern science that replaced superstition and gave us reliable *facts* about nature and our world. This knowledge was quickly put to use by many inventors to create industries that transformed the world.

SCIENCE HAS GIVEN US A MUCH BETTER LIFE

You are very fortunate to live at a most unusual time in history, in a country where very efficient methods of producing food and providing medical care keep most people alive and well long enough to reach old age in good health.

Nutritious food of astonishing variety is plentiful for most people in our country, but unfortunately, not for people who are poor or homeless.

In our nation, only one person in fifty is needed to work on farms, producing enough food for everybody else. Many kinds

Figure 10.1. A stream of grain pours from the spout of this gigantic harvesting machine. It does the work of hundreds of people. (John Deere Co.)

of powerful machines are available, each replacing the hard physical labor of many hundreds of people. (Figure 10.1)

We now have many large factories that produce huge quantities of a wide variety of different products. Most of the physical work is done by complex machines moved by electric motors. Thousands of different materials for industry and personal use are readily available that were not known before.

For energy we have fuels like oil, coal, and gas, as well as nuclear power and hydropower (water power). They move our cars, trucks, trains, tractors, ships, airplanes, and spaceships. They produce our marvelous electricity that operates motors to move machines in factories and appliances in our homes.

We can instantly communicate by telephone with people throughout the world. Millions of people can all see and hear events across the continent in their television sets at home.

We can visit places a hundred miles away by riding in cars or buses for just a few hours. In only five hours we can fly in airplanes across our wide continent, or go to any country in the world in less than a day. We can even send people to the moon and get them back safely.

BUT THERE ARE MANY HARMFUL EFFECTS

The scientific discoveries that have led to longer and better life have also led to the invention of immensely destructive weapons, especially nuclear bombs that could destroy civilization. Today's chemicals, fuels, pesticides, fertilizers, and wastes from many products pollute air, water, and soil.

The large quantities of goods we manufacture, then discard, end up as huge amounts of wastes that are rapidly filling garbage dumps and polluting water and soil. We are running out of space to safely dispose of our mounting wastes.

Increasing carbon dioxide in the air, produced as we burn immense amounts of fuels for energy, could cause "global warming." It is likely to produce harmful changes in climate, perhaps gradually flooding coastal cities as the warmed water in the oceans expands and the earth's ice caps melt.

The protective ozone layer high in the atmosphere could be destroyed by the chemicals used in refrigerators and air conditioners, by gasoline fumes, or by chemicals used in industry. Such a weakened ozone layer would allow more of the ultraviolet (sunburn) rays in sunlight to reach the ground and harm living things, including people.

The gasoline we burn in our cars pollutes the air and causes acid rain. Electric power plants that burn coal or oil produce useful electricity, but cause much of the acid rain that destroys plant and animal life in lakes and forests. Acid rain may also damage crops on our farms.

Nuclear power plants produce huge quantities of deadly radioactive materials. If released by accident, they can kill many people and make large areas of land uninhabitable for many years.

Nuclear power plants also produce dangerous radioactive wastes that last for many thousands of years. We have as yet found no sure way to protect future generations from these wastes.

For these reasons nuclear power is not as "clean" as many people think. It pollutes the environment, but in a different way than by burning fuels.

Modern medical care has saved many lives and greatly increased the average length of life. But in a number of undeveloped countries very high birth rates have caused overcrowding of the land, destruction of forests, overuse of farmland, and increasing poverty.

Forests are cut down for firewood, lumber, or paper. Overgrazing by cattle, sheep, and goats ruins grasslands and creates deserts. Farming in poor earth leads to erosion (wearing away) of soil. People are now changing the environment so fast that many forms of life have been destroyed.

A century ago people did not expect so many harmful effects from the results of scientific knowledge. People viewed "science" as all good. Today, however, many people are concerned that the harmful results of applying scientific knowledge may outweigh the good. They wonder if it would not be better to go back to the "good old days" when we did not know so much.

However, the same scientific *way of thinking* that has replaced superstitious thinking, and has given us longer and better lives, can also be applied to stop the harmful effects of science. How can we do this?

SCIENTIFIC KNOWLEDGE *CAN* HELP SOLVE OUR PROBLEMS

So far we have used scientific ways of thinking mainly to get new knowledge about *things*: materials (atoms and molecules), living things, energy (motion, electricity, heat, light, and sound), the earth, sun, moon, planets, and stars. We divide these studies into areas of knowledge like *biology, physics, chemistry, geology,* and *astronomy,* and its important uses such as *medicine, engineering,* and *architecture.*

Many people have become so expert at getting new scientific knowledge about *things* that we can now make rapid progress in solving very difficult problems in industry, engineering, and medicine. But it has proved much harder to discover and apply new knowledge about the *ideas* that cause *people* to do things that are now changing the world.

We are now beginning to learn how to do this in new sciences like *psychology* (how we think and behave); *anthropology* (origin and development of humans and their many cultures); *economics* (how we produce, distribute, and consume goods); *sociology* (the study of human society); and *political science* (how governments enable us to work together as communities, cities, states, and nations).

Developing these "people sciences" has been slower than for the sciences about "things." One reason is that when people are part of an experiment their own ideas, opinions, and different actions can change the observations others make. This often changes the conclusions for experiments. And those doing the experiments are also influenced by their own ideas and opinions.

Just the same, it is important to learn how to get new knowledge in these "people sciences" because everyone has an important part in solving the many troubling problems of modern society. As an example, consider how people could use scientific knowledge to solve the important problem of pollution and global warming caused by the burning of fuels.

AN EXAMPLE: HOW SCIENCE COULD REDUCE AIR POLLUTION

Our growing problem of air pollution is caused mainly by the burning of huge amounts of coal and oil in our cars, homes, and factories. We burn oil and gas to heat our homes; burn gasoline and diesel fuel for cars, trucks, trains, and ships; and burn mostly coal for our electric power.

Such burning puts huge amounts of sulfur dioxide and nitrogen oxides into the air, causing acid rain that destroys life in lakes and forests, makes people ill, contaminates soil, ruins the paint on homes and cars, and even weakens bridges.

Burning of coal, oil, and gas also puts carbon dioxide into the air that traps heat from the sun. This is very likely to make our globe warmer, thereby causing climate to change, the earth's ice caps to melt, and the ocean level to rise and flood the coasts.

From our knowledge of science we know a number of ways to reduce air pollution, and even to practically eliminate it some day. The two most important ways are: (1) *conserving energy* by using it *more efficiently* (using less energy to do the same work), and (2) replacing the burning of polluting fuels for energy with *non-polluting sources of energy*.

HOW TO CONSERVE ENERGY

Consider some of the ways we could use energy more efficiently so as to burn less fuel and reduce pollution. Better insulation would keep homes cooler in summer and warmer in winter. There would be less use of fuel and electricity, at lower cost.

We know how to make cars that travel twice as many miles for a gallon of gasoline than they now do. Fluorescent lights produce the same amount of illumination as incandescent bulbs with only one-third the amount of electric power.

Our industries can now manufacture more efficient furnaces, air conditioners, water heaters, refrigerators, and other appliances. Less electricity would be used and power plants would burn less coal and oil.

More efficient machines and appliances usually save people money, even though they may cost somewhat more money to buy. Costs for fuel and electricity are often reduced so much that the savings pay for the extra cost of the most efficient appliance in just a few years. After that the lower costs for energy save money year after year. At the same time less fuel is burned for power and this reduces pollution.

Why don't people buy the more efficient appliances that save money and reduce pollution? Most people do not know much about energy efficiency. When they buy homes or appliances, no one informs them how much money they might be wasting every year in higher costs for energy.

This requires *education,* not only of students in schools, but also of adults, especially the law-makers, leaders of industries, teachers, and reporters for newspapers and television.

We also need to develop ways to take into account the "hidden costs" of pollution caused by burning of fuels to supply energy. An inefficient car that wastes gasoline harms everybody because of the extra acid rain and global warming it causes.

The use of oil to make gasoline has also become one of the causes for wars over oil fields.

We need to take into account all those large hidden costs of coal and oil. If people had to pay for the pollution they cause by wasting energy, they would buy cars that use less gasoline, save them money, and reduce pollution.

We use many appliances in our homes that use energy: air conditioners, refrigerators, water heaters, lights, furnaces, cooking stoves, and electric heaters. All of them ought to have large labels that inform people about the cost for energy each year. Buyers could then compare the real cost of the inefficient, cheaper-to-buy appliances with the more efficient ones and save money by buying those that waste less energy.

Those inefficient, cheaper appliances could also be taxed to pay for the extra pollution, illness, and damage they cause.

Then they would no longer seem to be bargains and people would stop buying them.

Carefully designed laws by our government could also be used to help people conserve energy. For example, in 1973 there was an artificial shortage of oil that drove up the price of heating oil and gasoline to more than ten times what it had been before. That caused a severe economic recession.

In 1975 our federal government passed a number of laws to conserve energy and reduce use of oil. One law required automobile manufacturers to produce cars that burned fewer gallons of gasoline per mile. The automobile companies did not have to pay any extra tax if they produced efficient cars. But if they continued to produce energy-wasting cars they had to pay a large tax on each one they made. Manufacturers quickly produced much more efficient cars and our nation then saved huge amounts of oil.

Within ten years automobile manufacturers increased the average mileage per car from about 12 miles per gallon to 27. As a result, today's cars waste much less gasoline and cause much less air pollution.

Unfortunately, people became complacent when such energy-conserving actions caused the price of oil to drop. The government then relaxed its standards and car manufacturers no longer had to improve gas mileage. People began to buy larger, heavier, and more powerful cars, which used more gasoline. The campaign against energy waste almost stopped.

It is now possible for automobile manufacturers to produce cars that get an average of 40 miles for a gallon of gasoline. Raising the efficiency standards once again would save enormous amounts of gasoline and greatly reduce air pollution.

NON-POLLUTING WAYS OF SUPPLYING ENERGY

We can also greatly reduce pollution from burning fuels by replacing power plants that burn coal and oil with those that use non-polluting sources of energy. Energy from wind and sunlight are two forms of energy most likely to replace fuels in the future.

Windpower is now practical in many places throughout the world. (Figure 10.2) In the United States there is enough strong wind in twelve states of the Great Plains of our midwest to

Figure 10.2. Electricity is produced on this "windfarm" by an array of generators that are made to rotate by the wind. There is no pollution. Cattle can graze on the land around the wind machines. (Pacific Gas and Electric Co.)

provide all of our nation's electricity. Wind machines could be placed on many farms with little interference for grazing cattle and some kinds of crops.

We can produce electricity from sunlight in several ways. One method uses mirrors to concentrate sunlight, boil water, and produce steam to operate turbines and generators. Sunny deserts are ideal places for such "solar power" plants because uninhabited land is available at very low cost.

Another way of producing electricity from sunlight is with "solar electric cells." (Figure 10.3) Some special materials produce electricity whenever illuminated by light. In many areas flat sheets of such solar electric cells on rooftops of one-family homes could produce enough non-polluting electricity for all needs in that home.

One obstacle to replacing the burning of coal for electricity is that electricity from wind and sunlight now costs somewhat more to produce. However, the cost of energy from wind and sunlight is coming down very fast as improvements are made. It could be reduced even faster with "mass production" (production of many more wind and solar power plants).

Energy from wind and sunlight would also replace coal more quickly if the large hidden cost of pollution caused by using coal were added to the price of the electricity it produces.

Figure 10.3. This array of solar cells produces electricity from sunlight. In the future, 2 percent of the land area of all deserts in the world could produce enough non-polluting hydrogen fuel for all cars in the world. (Pacific Gas and Electric Co.)

Another serious obstacle is that wind and sunlight are not available whenever we want electricity. There are times when there is little or no wind and little electric power is produced. There is little sunlight on cloudy days and none at all at night. To solve that problem we need to have practical ways of storing the energy until it is needed.

This can be done with batteries, but they are still too expensive and heavy for most uses.

One good way of storing energy is to use the electricity from wind and solar power plants to produce hydrogen gas, an excellent, clean-burning, non-polluting fuel. This is easily done by sending electricity through water (electrolysis of water). The water molecules are broken apart into the separate hydrogen and oxygen atoms of which they are composed. The hydrogen can be stored in tanks for use as fuel for cars, home heating, and cooking. The non-polluting oxygen may be used for various industries.

Hydrogen is an ideal fuel because it is non-polluting when burned. All it produces is pure water, as steam, which does not produce acid rain, carbon dioxide, or pollute the air.

Hydrogen, or chemicals made from it, can also produce electricity in a device called a "fuel cell." Such fuel cells could use stored hydrogen in homes or local areas to produce electricity as needed.

Scientists are also working on ways to use the green chlorophyl in leaves, or chemicals like it, to use sunlight to produce clean fuels such as hydrogen.

All of these ways of producing hydrogen in non-polluting ways could some day completely solve our problems of using energy without polluting the air.

There are also other ways of getting non-polluting energy. Underground hot spots in the earth (geothermal energy) can be used to heat homes and produce electricity. Electric power could also be produced from tides, waves, and warm ocean currents (ocean thermal energy).

Such big changes in the way we get our energy cannot be made quickly. However, we could speed them up with more scientific research and development (experiments to make new devices more practical). If more scientists and engineers were put to work making improvements, we could greatly reduce or even eliminate air pollution much more quickly and save a lot of energy in the long run.

Each kind of energy has advantages and disadvantages that have to be weighed very carefully. Costs are important, especially the hidden costs that are now not taken into account.

EVERYONE CAN HELP SOLVE OUR BIG PROBLEMS

Everyone knows that the world now faces many difficult problems that will have to be solved as soon as possible. The big problems of pollution, overcrowding (population explosion), health, peace or war, drugs, and crime are all difficult to solve. But people who can think clearly, in every walk of life, have proved to be very resourceful in the past. We could use our wonderful brains in the future, as we have in the past, to solve many of today's problems.

Everybody has an important part to play in creating a better world. Whatever they happen to do for a living, as scientists, engineers, businessmen, workers, government leaders, economists, teachers, consumers, or citizens who vote, they can all help solve our problems. They will do it much more effectively if they learn to use scientific ways of thinking in which *facts*, not fairy-tale fiction, are used to make decisions.

You must not become discouraged. The human mind and the huge fund of knowledge we now have *can* be used to solve the difficult problems we face. But it will take hard work and good will by all of us to achieve that goal.

You do your part and set the example for others. Together everyone can help bring about a better world for all of us to enjoy.